From Chaos, with Love

Poetry from the Inside Out

From Chaos, with Love

Poetry from the Inside Out

Joshua Stutzman

Fresh Ink Group
Guntersville

From Chaos, With Love
Poetry from the Inside Out

Copyright © 2021
by Joshua Stutzman
All rights reserved

Fresh Ink Group
An Imprint of:
The Fresh Ink Group, LLC
1021 Blount Avenue #931
Guntersville, AL 35976
Email: info@FreshInkGroup.com
FreshInkGroup.com

Edition 1.0   2021

Cover design by Stephen Geez / FIG
Book design by Amit Dey / FIG
Associate publisher Lauren A. Smith / FIG

Except as permitted under the U.S. Copyright Act of 1976 and except for brief quotations in critical reviews or articles, no portion of this book's content may be stored in any medium, transmitted in any form, used in whole or part, or sourced for derivative works such as videos, television, and motion pictures, without prior written permission from the publisher.

Cataloging-in-Publication Recommendations:
POE023050 POETRY / Subjects & Themes / Family
POE023020 POETRY / Subjects & Themes / Love & Erotica
POE005010 POETRY / American / General

Library of Congress Control Number: 9781947893412

ISBN-13: 978-1-947893-41-2 Papercover
ISBN-13: 978-1-947893-40-5 Hardcover
ISBN-13: 978-1-947893-43-6 Ebooks

Dedication

*To my mother, Brenda,
and little princess, Riley Jean*

Delicacy Rules

On the battlefield of love delicacy rules,
Reflecting your needs while giving the tools.
Made with fragility and fanatically sought,
It's one of those things that just can't be bought.

So embrace the heart from the start,
Or watch it crumble and fall apart.
The goods, the bads, the ups, and the downs,
The ins and outs and all-arounds.

So realize love is a relic and not a gift.
It comes once a lifetime, feel the lift.
To look and search would be in vain,
And only bring on the showers of pain.

So be precise when you proclaim,
Because love's ritual is not a game.

Nothing is Limitless

I'll kiss Death on the lips
In the raindrops of misery,
Before I give up
A moment of history.

That we share
These flashes of Images,
Crushed in despair,
Nothing is limitless.

Raged with lunacy
A savaged chaos,
Sabotaged within
A sulking séance.

Needles of pain
Derived from flames,
A gaping hole
My heart's been maimed.

So let the sparks fly
Like shooting stars en route,
And never allow
Ours to fizzle out.

Blinding the Sun

The skies bleed water, a soothing thrum,
White fire flashes, blinding the sun.
Lulling and subtle, it strikes in stealth
Booming its might, showing its health.

Its beauty is harsh, an arrogant pose,
Like the thorn on a stem, found on a rose.
The grandest of sights you will see,
Drawn in the skies tactfully.

Spied at night, for a better view,
Streaks of light, a brilliant hue.
The tempered calm when daylight pours
Spitting its rays to warm the shores.

Spectral Things

Stained by the filth of love,
A spectral thing,
I should have stayed guarded
And kept you a fling.

Deep terrible sadness,
But nothing hurts forever.
We were all born to die;
From this life we will never.

Circling vultures
In the deepest pits of Hell,
Beauty found in the ugliest places;
The sleep of death is a spell.

Succumb to the sorrow
Like a relentless plague.
Lips tremble with disappointment;
It's for you they beg.

Dripping Revenge

The princess of pain and the man of steel,
With nightmarish frailty, vengeance is real.
My heart bleeds acidic gore,
Dripping revenge, my soul was tore.

Life is hard when you're doing time,
Making it better is easy unless it's mine.
I see the clowns, smiling in my face,
Though the entire time they wanna take my place.

Little do they know, I'm a beast, you can bet,
When I bring the heat, you'll see them sweat.
So pay your dues and debts of sanctity,
I'm the prince and sovereign, the king of misery.

Extravagant Views

Two stars lightyears away,
Twinkling bright, wanting to play.
Extravagant views in so many hues,
A rainbow during sunset let go of the blues.

Smile and let the warmth shine,
An amazing sight sending shivers down my spine.
Fondling my heart and inhaling my love,
Our souls entwined, fitting like a glove.

Abstract as quizzical art,
Never could I imagine being apart.
An intoxicating scent born on the breeze,
Never let down, you always please.

Velvet lips like an angel's kiss,
There's not a second I'd agree to ever miss.
I feel your embrace and hold it dear,
Reminiscing everything and keeping in clear.

Sanity Flew

Mocking the crazed with giggles of lunacy,

The gibberish spoken all too fluently.

A menacing tingle feel the surge,

The fringes of madness begin to merge.

Shattered hope of the helpless freak,

The psychotic shrill and endless shriek.

Willpower revealed and ground to grime,

Bitterness ensues the hands of time.

I've rampaged and scoured for the bliss,

The goal of life I pathetically miss.

Succumb to the calm that calls for you,

The irony is, sanity flew.

Precipice of Pain

Everything is said when you say nothing at all,

Is it futile to continue writing or call?

My heart hovers on this precipice of pain,

reluctantly I realize you're interjected with disdain.

This observation was easy for the world to see,

why I've been blind, thinking that you love me.

Benevolent I was, now receptive to the rage,

The chapters are substantial; is it time to turn the page?

Burned into my memory, an outrage, this is true,

diminishing a love that once was meant for you.

Love Flows

With a love as pure as freshly fallen snow;

and as ancient as the temples where the Mayans

used to go.

My colorful command of language, subtle and unique

but the way in which my love flows can never be oblique.

The audacity in which you gave my heart the boot,

gives the impression your feelings were always moot.

Fascinated by your charm and how you kept me hooked,

your dereliction is profound; you came for what you took,

Leaving me distraught, indignant to the pain

entirely, I've gone utterly insane.

Vikings

Let's hash it out like Vikings

and silence the screams with a sinister

smirk and a sickening gleam.

In pools of shadows fading to the night,

see the ethereal glow glinting in spite.

The poison runs deep and dwells inside,

in this jungle-ish habitat I'm with my pride.

From the curtain of stars emitting its light,

that lingering feeling something's not right.

So fathom the pain and the anguish dealt,

Pulsing in my veins you know it's felt.

See the intensity within my eyes,

bold yet humble, a warrior cries!

I Am Bane

In a battle of wits I'm a verbal assassin,

while they're standing still I blow right past 'em

Pullin' the trigger with these words,

killin' the nouns and slayin' the verbs.

In this realm I am Bane,

I took the crown, it's mine to claim.

So before you go against the king, remember

that this Monarch wears the ring.

I set the pace for you to follow,

good luck with this pill, it's hard to swallow.

So take a drink; I think you're choking,

from what I said, but I'm not joking.

Don't feel sad, or ashamed;

Lick your wounds—you've been maimed.

Unbound by Man

You're my inspiration, this is true;

flood gates have opened, you have no clue.

What you're capable of, you do not see,

and no, I don't mean figuratively.

Build me up or tear me down,

a blind man walking to lead me now.

To your lane of love, you wear the crown,

the palace of hearts I follow the sound,

covered in roses, your soft velvet skin,

seems like eternity, not being within.

Your garden of love, let's not pretend,

What my touch can do, no others can.

So feel your cheek within my hand,

the warmth we share like sun to sand.

Like riverlets of water together expand,

our love unbridled and unbound by man.

First of the Fallen

Wear the crown you claim on
the throne of lies, but heed
the warnings from a past that
cries.

With one foot in the gutter and
the other in the grave, when
karma comes calling the first of
the fallen are the Brave.

The war that rages within you can
be easily won, by planting flowers
on the grave of hate, growing in
the sun.

Live for the aroma of love, forgetting
the stench of despair;
this can be easily done as if it's
floating in the air.

She Peeks

Wrapped around her pinky,
A fool for her, I be.
With smiling eyes and a satiny voice,
a princess she is to me.

Innocent and pure,
amiably she speaks.
Snuggled with me when it's time for bed,
through hooded eyes, she peeks.

We would dance in the kitchen
and hold each other tight.
She's a queen among angels;
in the darkness she is light.

Just to watch her sleep,
I was lucky to see.
I failed to state her name,
But clearly it's Riley!

Heroic Resolve

Feel the depths of love within my kiss,

for you I yearn for and dearly miss.

Vibrant in color, a burst of warmth,

a watery image only beauty can warrant.

My heart races whenever you're near,

The sound of your voice I need to hear.

With a hint of peace and heroic resolve,

the passion is relished, the pain dissolved.

It is no more but the sky is gray,

I look to the heavens and begin to pray.

The pangs of guilt mocking and cruel,

battle cries of love follow the rule.

My heart has wilted in utter dismay,

the feeling is scarce but won't go away.

Passions

Back in love I fall, it's my mistress

whom I adore, she enfolds me in passion

while letting me explore.

Her body is inviting as she arches her back,

my Aphrodite in the flesh, her velvet curtains

are my snack.

Refusing to die is the lust that we share,

this love is unheard of; there is nothing to compare.

I want what she is, not what she could be;

her complexion is of cream and her desires rest with me.

She is a rider of the wind with crystalline eyes,

the interpretation of beauty and

her heart is my prize.

A Prophecy

Dancing in the kitchen seems to pale

to the thought of your smile that never fails

fills my soul like wind-a-sail,

or the stars in the sky that leave a trail.

Words mean nothing that is true

my heart's been captured and taken by you

as the moon comes up, the sun sinks down

dust from a back road, that familiar sound.

The song I sang that made you cry,

like your parents we can't deny.

This love we share is meant to be,

written in the stars a Prophecy.

With kisses like honey,

oh so sweet,

The one of my dreams that I was meant to meet

and so I did,

my queen she be,

I just can't believe she's chosen me.

In shambles I am a disastrous mess,

you're the glue that bonds me, I must confess.

Preludes to Love

My mind wanders in a Nirvana's mist,

velvety soft is your dainty kiss.

Lavender scrim in a softening sky,

wind chimes twinkle, a breeze passed by.

Seen from high terraces beauty rules,

mitigated by nothing my love pools.

That rippling infectious giggle

makes my heart soar,

perpetually obsessed, I shamelessly adore.

And I indefinitely admire the elegance in which,

your beauty keeps me frozen, in my heart

I feel the stitch.

Presumably regal, and I call you my queen,

the prelude is over, we've outlived the obscene.

Death Wish

In a cell is where I dwell,

With the smell of despair

"Welcome to Hell"

My death wish remains unanswered

and I don't know why,

On an endless sea of torment

I hang my head and cry.

This insurmountable urge

to pull the trigger on Life,

halitosis of the soul

smothered in strife.

So until Death calls for me,

it's revenge I seek.

My heart has been calloused

and is no longer weak.

Acquired Taste

Your dubiousness plagues my soul,

Discombobulated I am but never letting go.

I'm unlike other men that you've dated,

because I hit the spot leaving you sexually sated

And I'm preoccupied with how your hips sway,

my attraction's been driven in the strongest way.

I cannot mess around; I have acquired taste,

breathless anticipation as if I'm being chased.

That carnal activity burned indelibly on my brain,

with the swagger that I offer I know you can't refrain

from regaling in the memories

coyly looking back;

I've spoken about lust, but I love you—that's a fact.

Enticing the Wrath

A venal mind confides to the fiend his fear,

little does he know he speaks to himself,

looking in the mirror

with metaphors given, enticing the wrath,

feel the havoc in the giggles, and the malice

in the laugh.

The dark hound runs like strychnine in his veins,

and parasites fall into the corona of flames.

The practical logic rooted deep in disdain

it's radiating hate, like a crucifying pain.

Defiantly terse to the unsavory fanatic,

the roiling turmoil, conceited and sporadic.

Purplish Gray

A poetical bullet lyrically aimed at the insightful mind,

killing the hate while feeding love,

the unconditional kind.

Rage recedes, as affection radiates from the

beautiful soul, the mind concedes to the

compassionate touch, reaching its goal.

A summer's breeze answers the call with a warm embrace,

Purplish gray clouds on a baby-blue backdrop,

such a heavenly place.

So let me gaze just a little at a smile that shines,

The mold was broken when you were made

it's my heart that pines.

Devious Few

I'm at war with myself, and my
mind is at stake. Insanity growls
with every mistake…
Look at the weak as they cower
and cringe, into the abyss I'm
on the fringe.
Of the void as if I'm hovering,
within the elements
simply discovering.

The solitude within the storm,
where the thirst for revenge
was first born.
Now the disdain runs deep while
the revelation seeps, into my mind
with bounds and leaps.
With a defiant roar standing proud,
The devious few a rebellious crowd.
That captivity holds to no avail,
it's time we rethink this
thing called *jail*…

Flames of Love

The warm, desirable taste
of phantom lips kissing my heart.
An elegant magnetism
so persistent from the start.

The flames of love
licking my soul.
Irresistible devotion
paying the toll.

A broken whisper
with a boring stare
I need your touch
Like my lungs need air.

The distinction in which
I hold you above.
This astonishing analogy,
a persuasion of love.

Regrettably lost
what some feel is simple,
But I'd give everything
just to see that dimple.

Monstrous Lies

An arid love crumbles to dust, from being starved
of much-needed trust.
Grievous thoughts conquer the brain
intuitions an animal that needs to be slain.
But in this ball of self-pity it gradually
grows, love is a virtue that neither of us knows.
Wounds that don't close will never heal,
like the scab you keep picking and always
peel.
Impertinent we are when we believe that we're
Right; if I said I was sorry would it have
ended the fight?
But I realize we're mere mortals telling
monstrous lies, with precarious foreboding
where jealousy thrives.
Looking at me, your ambivalent feelings
show, but I've been planted in your life
and love's a thing to grow.

Unbound by Man

You're my inspiration, this is true

floodgates have opened; you have no clue

what you're capable of, you do not see,

and no, I don't mean figuratively.

Build me up or tear me down,

a blind man walking, so lead me now.

To your lane of love you wear the crown,

the palace of hearts I follow the sound,

covered in roses, your soft velvet skin,

seems like eternity, not being within.

Your garden of love, let's not pretend,

what my touch can do, no others can.

So feel your cheek within my hand,

the warmth we share like sun to sand.

Like rivulets of water, together expand,

our love unbridled and unbound by man.

The Squeal

Feathery soft kisses from you, I miss;

getting drunk on your taste is utter

bliss.

I can't explain how I've become so fond;

my capacity for forgiveness speaks of our

bond.

Those baby-blue half-hooded eyes,

that seductive giggle while I'm kissing

your thighs.

My tongue explores all your curves

and dips, that squeal of pleasure when

I nibble your hips.

Lightly licking and caressing your pearl

I pick up the pace and your toes curl.

Scream my name and dig at my back, the

beast of your beauty that's just a snack!

My Flow

A faint anger resides in your aura

and pulls us apart;

I could sense your transience almost

from the start.

The blatant inaccuracies that reveal

your resentment, you evade and equivocate

to achieve your contentment.

Tears to a river a continuous flow,

when will it cease,

maybe the day-breaking precedence

and achieving world peace.

But for now, retreat to the dark

with your cliquish retinue;

the fate of the world hangs heavy

on the shoulders of the virtuous

few.

Walled Away

Revenge is my mistress, and inflicting pain

is her goal,

with the hint of a smile and a gleam in her

eye she will take your soul.

The embarkation of misery in her perfunctory way,

inhaling her aroma while begging her to stay.

Anger creates destruction that's walled away

from trust, the sense of distance from your soul

doesn't compare to the lust.

So prattle about as she strips you to the bone;

her smile is false; she holds no love, this

she has shown.

Black as death is your heart, just look inside.

Run if you can and lock the doors; she's coming,

so hide!

Deceit Devised

Delusional thoughts of the slaughtered mind
The taint from the traitors left behind
Heaving adrenaline through my veins,
With twitching hysteria creating pains

This broken soul in a sea of madness
I've warred within this depraved sadness
A cursed whisper relentlessly cruel,
Shivering in shock stands the fool

Bizarrely thrilled as I grieve
Frozen in time, it does not leave
The deceit devised within the plan,
Furiously altered a humble man

A Feast for Eyes

Castles made of sand crumble over time;

My enigma you remain but the beauty is sublime

like a gentle summer's breeze or fruit on the vine.

Loving you is bliss, feeling your fingers entwined with mine.

Blinded, but I see, my eyes feast on your features,

The compass of my life, I forget all other creatures.

with your hazelnut-brown eyes and toffee-colored hair,

Like moonlight on the waves, I cannot help but stare.

Snuffing the Light

We are not a civilized species;
We are all of us savages on the cusp of extinction,
Jumping from one mate to the next,
Spreading disease, forgetting distinction.

Compassionless mothers kill their sons,
to go out at night,
While monstrous fathers rape their daughters,
Snuffing a mind that was bright.

Recycling deformities of the mind,
Causing these defects of the soul.
Abominations unknowingly created with a vision
That's darker than coal.

Salute

Look into the eyes of this hellish beast,

where red-hot rage and flames feast.

When the soul's gone numb and vacancy lives,

the howls release like a sieve.

Morbidly grim with a corrosive stench,

salute my soldiers who do not flinch.

Smeared in the blood of those found weak,

ending in cries of a strangled shriek.

Tossed away mangled and torn,

absently bitter and full of scorn.

With a boisterous roar, the end is near;

you're in the cobwebs of hell, engulfed in fear.

Born from Sin

The grime of crime stains my name,
Yet the brightest of futures is mine to claim.
I faltered from doubt creeping in;
Paranoia, my ruin was bred within

And reunited with a grief born from sin,
I'm terrifyingly calm in the din.
The stakes are high, the blueprint was laid;
The devoted roar to stop the charade.

Now rant and mumble, claw and bite,
But where you stand is in my sights,
And the gesture you gave played the tune
To tell me the end was coming soon.

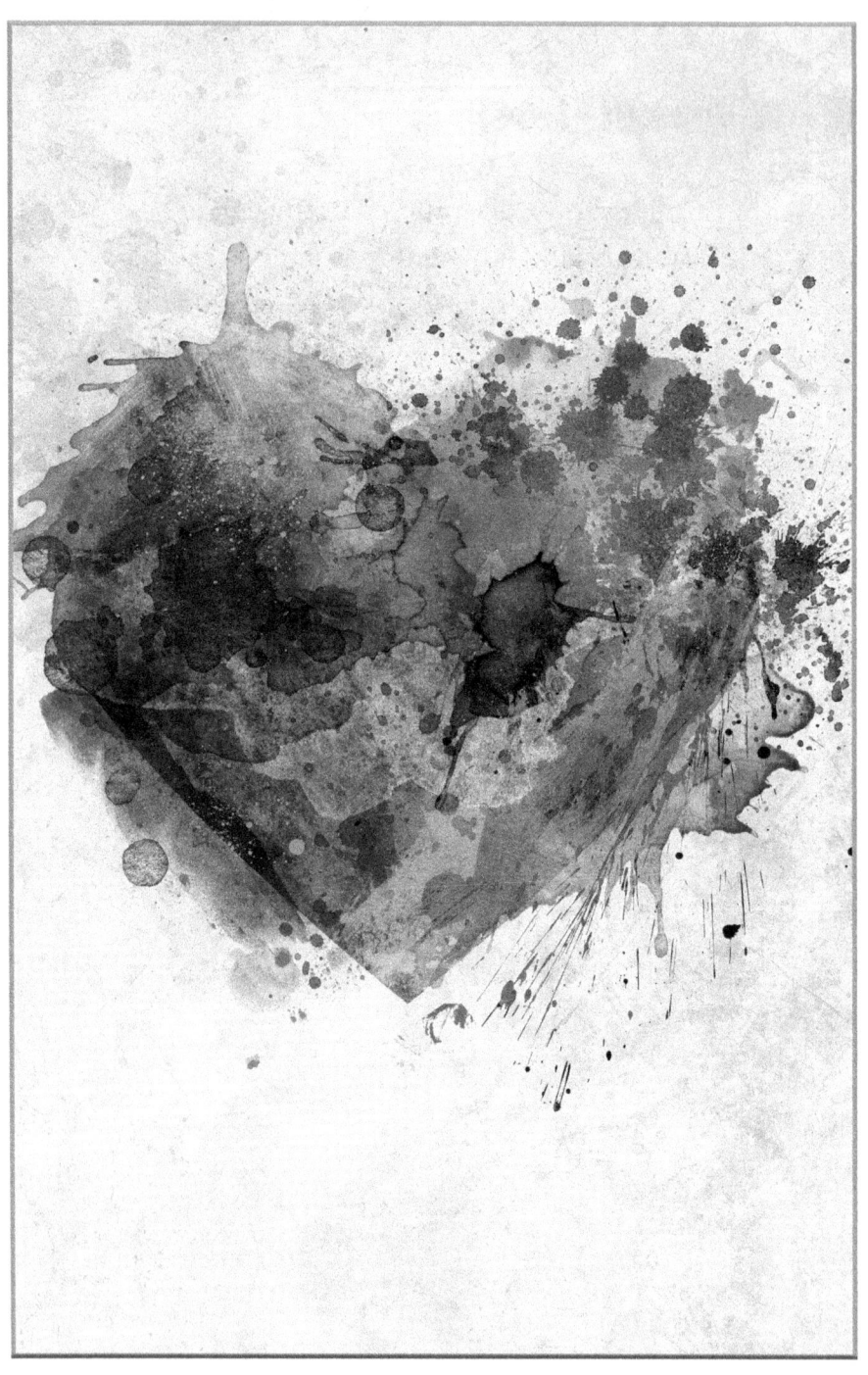

Contours of You

Gingerly embracing the contours that is you,
See the excitement in my eyes that's long overdue,
Tenderly caressing with an entangling touch,
A lullaby of pleasure executed as such.

An infamous love grown from a seed,
Infatuated, I am, absolutely indeed.
In a torrent of lust where pheromones fly,
When these hormones kick in, you'll tell the others goodbye.

The temptation you bring is staggering, at best.
Getting what I want means you'll get no rest.
I'm entitled to you and you to me;
Being together, we've been set free.

Absurd Conundrums

Is too much love as bad as no love at all,

especially in a world where loyalty is law.

Picasso of my time but only with words,

an abstract lyricist, the conundrum's absurd.

You mess with me and you're going to get beat,

an excellent flavor but damn sure not sweet.

This obnoxious context easily merged

like electric currents, the power surged.

Quaintly woven with a tentative touch,

with an iron fist, this crown I clutch.

Whiskey On Ice

Fire-filled constellations held in spite
In a majesty of love on this night,
Eyes sealed shut, closed up tight
Like doors in a prison, that's my plight.

Lightning bugs dancing between you and I,
Unequivocal epiphanies in a star-filled sky;
There is no other I could ever see,
No woman but you, I pledge to thee.

A heart that's true will never die.
I'm sorry if ever I made you cry.
I'd drink those tears, that's no lie
Like whiskey on ice made with rye.

I've grabbed heaven's ear
To tell of the fear
I have of hearing
The word *goodbye!*

A Ravenous Hunger

A love underestimated like the darkness before
light, infused with orgasmic ecstasy loving the
fight.
Eager anticipation consuming the fear, it's this
ravenous hunger I feel when you're near.
So as I sit, and take a meditative breath,
I realize that losing your love might as
well mean death.
The enchantment you laid was impeccably divine,
graceful with rhapsodies so romantically in line.
Now in converging on your succulent lips
to steal a kiss, endearing with your tone, I'm
living in bliss.
Now I'm anchored in your life,
regardless of your strife, relinquish your
last name to become my wife.

Shivering Madness

Wisdom, a notion vanished from sight,
awakened the instincts colliding with fright.
Excitedly laced with a choked gasp,
the ante's been upped,
a speechless rasp.
Relief seeps in and finds solidity,
only to be ravaged by humility.
With blissfulness gone in endless days, and stifled cries from
unstable ways.
In this blanket of dark a fog of blackness,
twinkling bright a shivering madness.
An undeniable impulse swelters
in the ashes, melting in irony
derived from the clashes.
Risen from karma, drawn towards the clouds,
survival of the fittest,
thin out the crowds.

Instincts Rot

Humanity weakens in the coils of pain,
Tears glisten, leaving their stain.

Heinous spirits resist the light,
sullenly dull and massing to flight.

With fire in my veins, vile and hot,
a false hope lingers and instincts rot.

The bloodthirsty try to quench their thirst;
I won't be faded, as I shoot first.

Hear the slurs from the strewn who crumble;
in agonizing defeat they frantically mumble.

A gnawing filthiness foreign and slight,
it's done on a whim and done in spite.

I'm the savior of bane and I do claim,
with an iron fist I was born to reign.

Savage Grin

Within the lion's lair, I lay,
cast aside to the pits of hell,
I must pay.

Hideous fear from pain, endured a broken soul;
the lore and gore from warped minds has
taken its toll.

Incomplete and damaged, the pain is mine along with madness;
the constraints of compassion no longer hold
the certainty of sadness.

Falling deeper into a sea of despair with a savage grin,
squeals of rage, a shrieking litany is
born of sin.

His lips are twisted to a sinister smirk,
morbidly looking with bloodshot eyes and
a sardonic quirk.

Demented Ecstasy

Grasping for straws in the wind as thunder booms,
and seeing the crackling lightning as it consumes
and threatens the majesty of the snow-capped kings,
pelting its power, driving its strings.
In this war for dominance, brutally I reign.
This inward torment is driving me insane.
Hear the frantic echoes with craziness laced,
demented ecstasy claiming its place.
As the dreaded storm on the horizon seems
To throw shards of white light so brilliantly seen,
With a tangible presence and a creepy moan,
the turmoil is yours, so reap what you've sown.

Decadent Taste

Hearts break and the tears seep,
pulling back into black, yearning
for sleep.

Vulgar and violent and amazingly cruel,
Terrifyingly beautiful while
playing the fool.

The comfort you seek comes with the flames of hell,
alone and hollow, nothing left
but a shell.

The sweetness of Death, a decadent taste,
sacrifices for love are
given in haste.

Everything is taken and all seems lost,
blinded by rage not
knowing the cost.

So when love cost you everything and cast you away,
love yourself at the end
of the day.

Thankful

You can put out the flame,
but the coals still burn.
Everything is what it isn't
when the tables are turned.

I desire the meaning
at the cost of Death.
It's at the end of suffering
that you catch your breath.

No longer bound by
hate or chained with rage,
the curtains have closed.
I'm leaving the stage.

Thankful for life and
the joys I get,
for the bonds unbroken and the
time that we get.

If nothing remains, but
the words I leave,
read between the lines in
the web that I weave.

Echoes

My thoughts equate nothing as I sit and dream.
Looking to the skies,
I silently scream.
Trust has become a weapon to slay your soul,
said once but forever heard,
taking its toll.

You eased out of love—I no longer exist—
dripping insanity like blood
from my wrist.
Emotionally drained, and the tears run free,
through the twists and the turns, there's
nothing to see.

The wind echoes your name as I fight for a breath,
Blended from love and wishing for death.

Stars

I'm like the stars in the
sky, in a way. At a glimpse,
I'm close, yet a million miles
away.

Burning bright from within,
a magnificent sight, yet set
to implode with a devastating
might.

My heart has been sheltered
within walls of pain,
chaos shattering the love and
leaving it slain.

Untouched, untainted, and
wildly untamed, the beauty
erasing the skies has been
maimed.

Chaos

With the enemies of light
and love against, comes chaos,
pain, and betrayal sensed.
Prisms of Pain, the color of
Darkness; the saint of demons
relishes the heartless.
In the heart of winter the
cold wind blows; open the
door and come in from the
snows.
Dreams have their logic, can
we agree? The madness inside
is lunacy.
This hate that comes from
within was placed by the
one committed to sin.
With the mighty betrayer's
tiniest smirk, ungodly chaos is
his darkness at work.

The Brink

For a glimpse into hell, just
follow me, down a spiral of
insanity to an ominous sea…

The harsh stare from the
mask of misery, or fickle
smirk given so vividly,

Where the eerie silence is
broken by a gurgling scream, and
the haunted souls provide a ghastly gleam.

See the fear frozen in a
hideous scowl; welcome to Hell
—some call it the bowel.

Vicious obscenities pour from a
demonic beast, covered in
blood from its sadistic feast.

With oblivion seen in just a
wink, let's all go swan dive
past the brink.

Kissing the Sky

Losing the battle within, can someone remind me who I am? All I know is it's dark, and hell is hot—this must be a sham.

I scream at the heavens, give me back my soul, hear my hoarse cries, I've paid the toll.

Nothing else matters but kissing the sky, with a dimly lit view, in the abyss, I lie.

I know I'm lost. There is a debt to be paid, but I know not the cost.

Spilling my heart with a bloody pen, we all get dirty, even the best of men.

Magnificent Nomad

Circumventing my heart, a hasty
defection, magnificence named
of love's inflection.
Cold as snow and half past
crazed, the guttural sounds
come from the haze.
A poisonous weed grows within
my brain, lashing at my will,
blocking out the pain.
See the searing agony my
eyes do hold; you can't be
saved from yourself, so I'm told.
An indescribable torment is humming
inside, adoringly morbid and
straining to hide.
A slave, I've become, because
I professed, a venomous touch,
A deadly caress.

Souls Sold

I sold my soul—can I buy it
Back? I'll give you twice what
you paid, even though it's black.
Fossilized and lame it's integrity's
Lost. I was given but a fraction
of its actual cost.

Pure, it's not, and through the mud
it's crawled; I've misspent my life enormously flawed.
I'm almost home—I've found my
way—with my soul intact, I'll eagerly pay.
When I sold my soul for what I thought was a
home, I really sold my soul just to be alone.

Accepting Fate

When I die, I accept my fate, Whether I'm alone or in the arms of my mate. I've lived by the gun to die by the knife Ironic, I say, is this thing called Life. I look to the skies as if that's my goal. I fill one up while digging a hole. The good and the bad. I've seen it all. The only thing I've missed is a lover's call. In the throes of death, I'm finally free from this battle I wage with Insanity.

Pluto

Pinks and purples highlight the sky,
that sinking sun that blinds my eye.
Once we shared this view of hues,
it's no longer mine—I don't get to use
its beauty and power to summon the love
from my queen, my turtle dove.
I taste what I cannot have,
your intoxicating scent, hearing you laugh.
The setting of the sun, my desire,
it's the color of your hair—that of fire

Do you dream of me as I do you?
It can't be so; you have no clue
how much I care. I dare you, too,
but you'll never come close to my love for you.
So as the sun sets and the light winks out,
the moon takes over, you know I'm about.
To say I love you there and back,
Pluto's my goal, that's a fact.
I say this to you again and again,
I'll love you forever and ever.

Amen.

Yours to Claim

Take my hand as well as my name.
Take my heart; it's yours to claim.
I'll hold you gently like a feather
in wind; in a hazy cloud of
love you can't comprehend
what I see when I look at the moon,
and in my dreams an impending doom.

But my faith is strong, feel my kiss.
With a heart so true, can I miss?
I know tempers run hot and angers flare.
At the end of the day, I'm going nowhere.
So as the sun sinks and you look around,
Think of me. I wear the crown.
Your aura does shine, brighter than gold.
I'll carry that weight, it's mine to hold.
The hunger I have will never die,
You are my rib, apple of my eye.

Fate

In a chainless trap that never lets go,
I'm enslaved, from the doubt in my heart and pain in my soul.
I am bathed.

It's a split second, yet feels like years,
the poetry of fate unspoken,
yet heard through tears?

Like raindrops tapping on a window pane,
how much love can be given
before going insane?

The emotions well and burst the dam,
fighting for breath,
drowning I am.

The sweetest taste to be had
is from the kiss of Death.
This is sad.

Mending

Beauty is held in the
eye of the beholder, and
what I see is pure: There's
no easy way to mend a
broken heart; that is for sure.

Vulnerability displayed and
has been shown from the
start, your Trojan Horse
of love got through my
defenses and destroyed
my heart.

The consternation felt
like a sharp, stabbing pain, and
tears vanish into the soil
just like the rain.
Now blood seeps from a
heart that's been broken
and torn, with an outpouring
of emotions.
Your love is a scorn.

No More Goodbyes

The sun sinks down into the sand,
with a warm breeze, blowing across
this land.

As the moon comes up, I take your
hand. This love we share
is in demand.

By the gods in the galaxy,
they heard my prayer
and my plea.

So now I live on bended knee;
you are my queen,
you set me free

From my past and help me learn,
that even the broken
deserve a turn.

Now take me home where love
is sown, in the North
where I was grown.

And as the leaves turn and
summer cries, you're my one and only—
no more goodbyes.

Riley's

Blond hair and bright blue eyes,
Dad's saving grace, it's no surprise.
I remember when you first
came home, the snuggles shared,
the love that was shown.

On my chest you'd fall asleep,
the pitter-patter of little feet.
You'd mumble these words and it was sweet,
"my little love-bug."
Aren't you neat?

I'd play with your hair every night,
until you'd snore,
eyes closed tight.
Light up my life with a laugh
you stole my heart,
it's yours to have.

My princess, you are, and a queen
you'll be. I know you're confused
and missing me.
These are all things that are meant to be.
Daddy's coming home;
you will see!

Out of Reach

When what you want most
is right in front of you, yet
completely out of reach,
there's a silver lining in every cloud—
at least that's what they teach.
Love is paramount, but it seems I'm immune,
defying the onslaught,
not hearing the tune.
From million-dollar dreams to lonely nightmares
absorbing your love and drinking your tears,
at the door to heaven,
yet standing in hell; life's a
paradox, I can finally tell.
I'm drowning in a pool of misery
and shame; gaze into my eyes—
at midnight you can see the flame.

Free in Life

Like a sparrow in flight, it's an eye's
delight, so graceful and sleek—but
nothing compared to the mountains
in May with their snow-covered peaks.
Or how about the mist that hangs
in the air without a care, and the
shooting stars that light the sky
while you stare.

With the sun shining on the grass
covered in dew, and the moonlight
glow surrounding your love in a
beautiful hue,
all of these things are free
in life yet rarely seen, at least until
it's too late, it would seem.

One Last Kiss!

Fiery orange with the softest pinks,
yellows and blues in a sky that sinks.
In this backdrop I do see, the woman
I love unconditionally.
Whispery sweet, I hear your call, seeking
your face or none at all;
lips so warm and full of life, the
sharpest tongue as if a knife.
Pale as the moon, and white as
pearls, your flawless skin
with silky curls.

Those baby blues and soft pink lips,
manicured toes and fingertips.
A love beyond what either has
known, I'd sacrifice all this
I have shown.
Vanishing deep into the abyss, but
before I go,
one last kiss.

Eradicated

Leaving rose petals on the
grave of our past, saying
goodbye to a love that
was meant to last.

Saying "So long" to a world we knew,
as the images fade,
the ugliness in you exposed
by the games you played.

Eradicating my thirst for love,
sadness mingles with pain.
I must be cursed, as this
constant torment has left its stain.

So dance with the demons
and shower in shame; as
the scars rip open,
only your self is to blame.

Fringes of Forever

As the sun starts to rise,
turning the sky a pinkish blush; looking
into the eyes of the woman I love
my heart starts to rush.
On the fringes of forever,
my mind begins to swirl, and I think
to myself the beauty in the
sky has nothing on my girl.
It's impossible to explain
what holds me so captivated and stuck,
I've been enraptured by your scent,
to claim your lips was just luck.
Crippling is this thing called love,
but somehow it finds a way,
just like that pinkish blush
blessing in the sky from the sun
each day.

Wracked Emotions

Throw me to the wolves
and I'll lead the pack.
Make sure if you do,
that you don't look back.

As the echoing screams
pierce the night,
feel trickling fear,
brought on by flight.

See hideous monsters
with twisted faces,
apocalyptic thoughts,
in nightmarish places.

The crestfallen demeanor
of the beaten coward,
with tired eyes and racked emotions,
fierceness is powered.

So ready or not
here I come.
It's a war of the worlds,
on a planet of one.

Treason

Incapable of being loved for
whatever reason, some things
are unforgiveable, including your treason.

Sullen and petulant, my
tears wash away the sorrow; love today
with all you have, you might not get tomorrow.

Passionately embraced, this solitude
of death; in a flood
of premonitions I feel the dragon's breath.

The void that was created
permeates my soul; I remain
the captive, which I believe was your goal.

Embrace the Chaos

Roses are dead and
the violets are too;
in a world gone cold
I embrace the chaos that is you.

Exceeding understanding
and stained by hate,
from treachery to misery
I'm living my fate.

An endless sleep
is what I crave,
a mummified body to
be laid in the grave.

A bristled brain;
blood, sweat, and tears;
in perpetual darkness
I face my fears.

The Beauty I Bring

Make me a caterpillar and let me
crawl to impossible heights, yet
never to fall.

In this ruthless world where
pandemonium is king, beauty is the
one thing I'm meant to bring.

Under a leaf you may find me,
quietly munching, feeling divine, an enigma
to you; yes it's true, for only I know what to do.

When the seasons change and
it's time to go, I'll be bundled up
against the snow.

So do not touch and you will
see, come next spring what
I'll be.

When I wake up to the warming
sun, watch me closely;
I'm almost done.

So again I say it's beauty I
I bring; make me a butterfly and
let me sing.

Traces of Me

I'll sing you a melody and seduce
your mind, your body and mine
with a bottle of wine.
Like a comb to hair, a tangled
pair, in the sheets feel the
flare.

The depths of my love can't be
reached, it's not in a book and
can't be "teached."
Feel my touch, invisible hands, the
soft sound of sleep, like tracks
through sand.

With traces of me left in the
air, slight they may be, but
they are there.
That beacon of beauty brings
tears to my eyes, with a
comforting sense, an elated surprise.

Delusions I clung to, immaculate
poses; I'll cover the bed with
petals of roses.

Moonlight Love

In the purple traces of dawn
I sit and ponder
about elaborate emotions that
constantly wander.

With toxic explosions amongst
waves of pleasure, the
moonlight illuminates my
life's endeavor.

My love's a fire that never
burns out; with writhing
flames of ecstasy, it leaves
no doubt.

To the pale luminescence
shone in twilight, to the
intimate salvation that lives in
the night,

when your lust manifested
and awoke my love, for
those crystalline eyes I'd place no
one above.

In a room dimly lit, I'm in
a daze; looking at you, I
stand amazed.

Does Love Fade

Can you remember the taste of my
kiss, your breath I'd take in utter bliss?
—the midnight rains that lightly mist,
with sounds of thunder from heaven's fist.

I've seen the sun in the midst of rain,
a few more drops I'd love to claim.
Our hearts beat harder, the closer
we are; I promise my love is up to par.

Waves give life to the moon, as if
angels are in the room.
I feel them crash into me—who
would have thought we would be?

My heart broke with the sun; on top
of temple it was done.
The sight of tears held me numb, to hear
you think, you're not the one.

The crack in my heart expressed in voice;
look in my eyes and see them moist.
Life is filled with actions we choose,
the one in my life I refuse to lose.

Roses and violets in all their vibrance,
with leaves that shade the color of jade.
Like our names on skyline,
does love fade?

Loyalty Over Love

Loyalty over love, it's a way of life
and how to live. I dimly remember a
reversed scenario and how I'd forgive.
I lost myself to find the man I
am today, unspeakable losses from
the sacrifices I had to pay.

I jumped in head-first, despite the
signs, tiptoeing on eggshells
and sidestepping mines.
I could see the hate infusing your
Soul; it consumes your life and
takes a toll

On us all, and we become deranged,
dismembering ourselves and
ignoring the strange.
Call it a malady, call me insane,
I've spent a life searching for love
I could never obtain.

Twisted Steel

My life's a movie and yours is an
episode, so get out the way—
you're stepping on toes.
I'm 200 pounds of twisted steel,
looking to relieve, not giving
two squirts of piss, please
believe.

I can't show love because
I have no heart; I've been
kicked while down and
broken apart.
Now I'm solid, just like cement;
you should have known that was meant.
To be a prodigy, a spectacular
sight, blinded by greatness,
bathed in light.

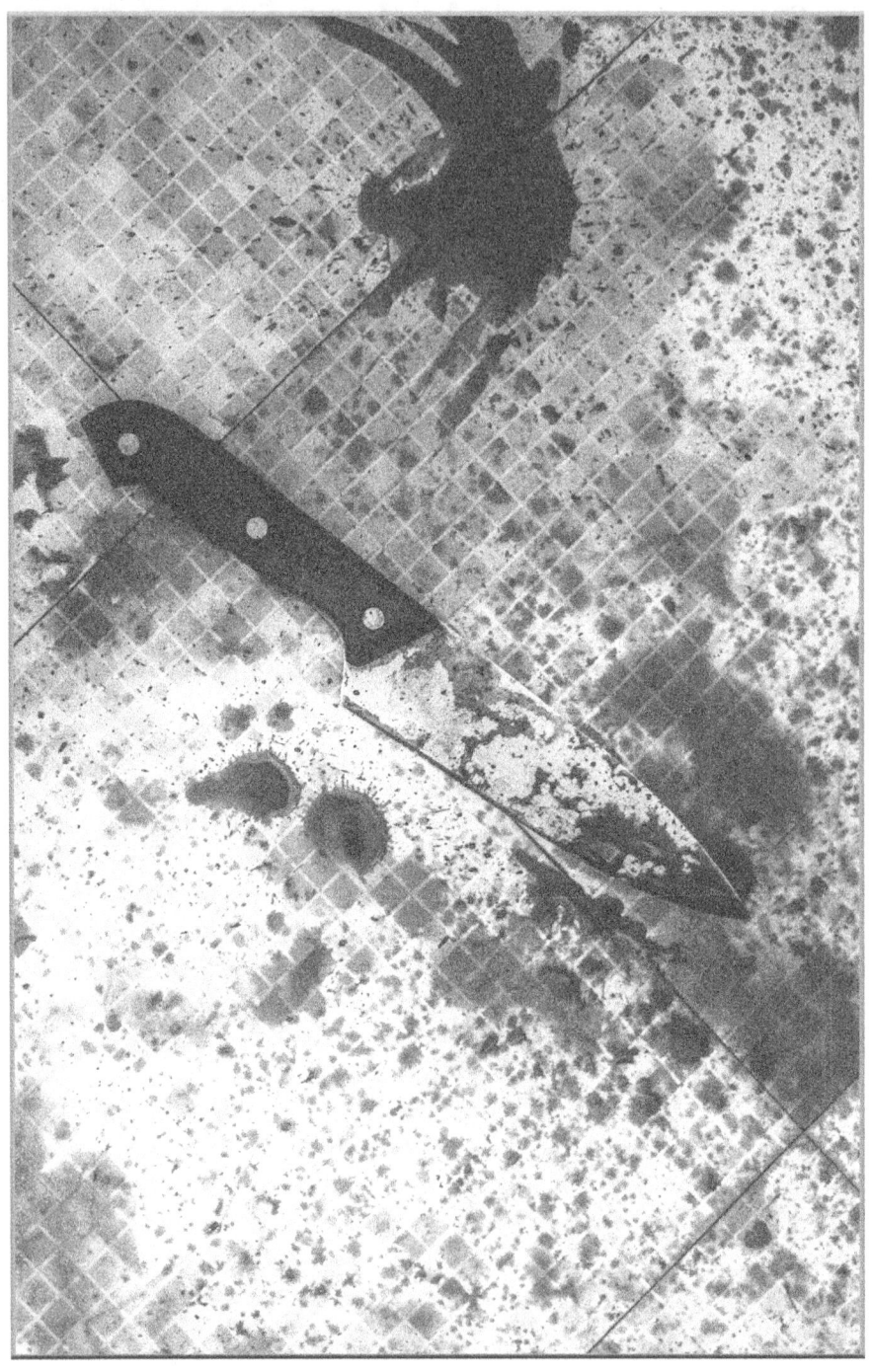

Prices to Pay

Blood drips from the knife
you used on the night
I died; curiosity sparked
but you snuffed it out,
from love you hide.
Set in sorrow my
heart's been inlaid; it's
good to be king but there's
a price to be paid.
Premonitions prophesized and
deceptions became clear;
the degrees of your falsity
make you a graduate of fear.
The disguised deceiver has
a halo of fire; you can't
long hide your lies while
retaining desire.

Goodnight

We live on the edge, so when it
rains it pours; come back from the cusp
to the indoors.
Now take that step to fall back in love,
the sacred feeling of
turtledoves.

Cardinals and blue jays flying free—
It's the perfect example of how
we should be.
Feel the tingle of the rush; with
the tip of my tongue I'll make you
gush.

Oops—I'm sorry I meant to say *blush*,
but under my touch your
body is mush.
In darkness, we were, but check
your sight; as I say this to you, I love you—
goodnight!

Metaphors Tried

In an everlasting lake of fire,
every tear will be dried, with the misguided
tendencies of metaphors tried.

Blinded by grief and too numb to
care, that the gnashing of teeth
fills the air.

A compassionate love for badness
and sin, it's unutterably beautiful
and hidden within.

The passions of life, the
cynical fruit; despondent I am,
self-hatred is moot.

Anarchy is here and it's time
to choose, so let me cut to the chase, men of
mayhem don't lose!

Beautifully Ignorant

A delicate flower rotting in the
sun, to the core its petals come
undone.

Blown away by the winds of an
Autumn's breeze, the leaves have
died too; look at the trees.

As they fall and kiss the earthen
sky, it's these morsels I miss,
and how they vie.

Towards that amber sheen, they
do ascend, beautifully ignorant
until the end.

I approach these things with
frivolity, not comprehending how
precious they be.

This enchantment returns year upon
year; their beauty is bright,
vividly clear.

Smell their scent in the air—
who would have thought
I would care?

1,000 Deaths

Anger and hate have torn you
apart, but your smile alone
lights up my dark.

Stumbling in my quest and
losing my soul, right to
yours and never let go.

There's no second chances,
only the now; mistakes
cost lives, I've been shown how.

Truer words have never been
Spoken; my heart has hardened
since you left it broken.

Churning whirlpools
of pain, trying to catch
my breath.

To losing you, I'd rather die
One-thousand deaths.

Give Up the Light

Today I've broken, succumbed
to disdain; my heart has
been murdered and been left
slain.

I give up the light to see
in the dark; you set me
on this path from which I
embark.

Losing my mind, my heart
and soul, everything is
cold and black as
coal.

Numb my mind and let
despair reign, we are all of us
tainted; everyone is
insane.

Sucked back into the nightmare
excruciatingly aware, enveloped
by the darkness, and you don't
care.

Frozen Flames

Dripping irony like a frozen
flame, a lifeless black,
but its breath I claim.
Concealed rage enshrouded
in hate, endlessly instant,
twisting your fate.
Lashing out, to swallow the
pain, with a ragged grin
and a blood-soaked stain.
Pervaded insanity like a
moth to light, the warmest
recollections were before I
could fight.
The faintest of smiles that
one could see have been
irreplaceably lost and stolen
from me.

A Notion

See the moon and think of me,
As I do you eternally.
Minutes to hours and those to days,
Thoughts of you, plays and plays.
I see you spy through fluttering eyes;
the hint of lust is my prize.
Your taunting scent gives me chills,
like a gusting wind on the hills.
Just like old lovers tried and true,
They know exactly what to do.
And like the waves in the ocean,
It can't be measured.
My love's a notion.

Tenderly Hold

My declaration of affection borne on the wings of love,
eyes mad with passion that's been sent from above.
You're my harbinger of heaven on earth,
this manifestation you've known from birth.
My precious beloved from first sight,
inevitably devoted like darkness to night.
I take my romance like I take my rye,
on the rocks with a watery eye.
There's a myriad of men who wish to be me,
but the mundane attempts made you see.
So tenderly hold this docile heart,
as it's belonged to you from the start.

I Think

I think of you in my arms and how you felt,
I think of your taste and how you smelt.
I think of how alone I am and break inside,
I think of the joys of love I'll no longer hide.

I think of you thinking of me,
Thinking of us, and what we could be.

I think you knew,
the pride I felt to be in your life.
There was no doubt the tears ran freely;
you became my wife.

You're in my thoughts through noon and night,
Like a soul clad in gold, such a spectacular sight.

Deformed and Contorted

Finally free to forget feeling, and my heart grows cold once again;
Mischievous inflictions in the bowels of hell is where I begin.
Your gullible acts and harsh ridicule has made me flee,
Like dissipated mist, your rebellious sarcasm casts an evil glee.

Deformed and contorted now revealing your hate,
The potential I see you've used as bait.
Melting towards the sky, my soul is ripped;
your pronouncement of love comes poisonous tipped.

Your blade protrudes from the back to the front;
glistening in the flames my heart was the hunt.

To the Most Understanding Person in the World

Who's the one who carried you and gave you a name,
the one you puked on, yet she loved you the same?
Who's the one you needed when your knee was scuffed;
you put on a brave face but she called your bluff?

Who's the one who worked, cooked, and cleaned,
who got you to school and everything in between?
Who's the one you call when times are rough,
who's always there when things get tough?

Who's the one in your life who never turned away,
even when it seemed your love went astray?
The one I speak of, a saint she be;
It's a mother's love that sets you free.

Sleight of Hand

My hummingbird frozen in flight,
but the terms of your love
vanished from sight.

Sparsely given with a sleight
of hand, the purest emotion
known to man.

My goddess of love delivered
by fate, boldly taking what's
on her plate.

The rapturous touch of my
queen, her golden gleam
can be seen.

With the mottled image
eccentricity posed, but through my eyes I
see a rose.

With a mischievous smile
tenaciously given, for you I breathe and
keep on living.

Enemies Lust

The sporadic urge, a mutating disgust,
when the friend of a friend of an enemy lusts,
it reveals the monster built up inside.
The friend of an enemy's enemy should hide.

You're abruptly powerless and on the verge,
with a fireball of rage that seeks a purge.
This apprehensive fiasco comes to an end,
so intentionally spoken you can't comprehend.

The quiet warning with menace inside,
contagiously spreading it will never subside.
So abandon the hope to win this war;
you have no idea what is in store.

Silence the Scream

The beast within fights to control;
on my mind it takes its toll.
Frantically grasping for a glimpse of sanity,
eccentrically screaming life's profanity.
From the mountaintops, I reign,
this crown of shit filled with pain.
I've lived a life filled with shame,
the mistakes I've made,
I take the blame.
I will not cry, nor complain;
walked through fire and felt the flame.
I'm still winning, but what's the game?
—a rolling stone you cannot tame.
Bolts of lightning in pouring rain,
the thunderous sounds on demon's plane.
With claws like razors and teeth that gleam,
In hell we are ,it would seem.
Wake me from this nightmare or dream,
and tell me it's over—
Silence the scream.

Hell to Pay

A guilty man cuts the string and falls away
from the life that he knows; there's hell to pay.
Dues are owed—where do I pay?
Down below,
Where it's hot, he likes to play.

In the flames with the demons you chose to keep,
don't play the tune;
do not cry;
Please don't weep.

Now your soul is gone;
it's his to have.
You gave it up,
signed it over;
hear the laugh.

So cower and bow to your King;
Pledge your fealty.
Swear an oath
and kiss the ring.

Mourn

Do not mourn for me;
mourn for love lost that was truly meant to be.
Mourn for the loyal who fought and tried;
mourn for the honesty that died from the lies.
Mourn for the lovers who were kept apart;
mourn for the tears in a broken heart.
Mourn for those who lose their way,
knowing they're not loved back and still, they stay.
So mourn for me, maybe you should,
for all I've described, I've lived and still, I'm misunderstood.

Reject

Progressively hated, just a casualty of life,
the agony radiated from the poison tipped knife.
Betrayed trust, you can smell it in the air.
Everyone else goes on as normal;
no one seems to care.

Living in purgatory every day is the same,
living in madness derived from the pain.
Failure is what I know and I've come to expect.
No matter what I do,
I'm just another reject!

Devilish Cycle

Introverted and diseased to the core,
with a suicidal rage I let it pour.
Deeply damaged, a tremendous despair,
this devilish cycle just isn't fair.

Reclusive, I live to perish alone,
contorted intimacy that I have shown.
Overshadowed by doubt, my ego's in pain,
the agonies of searching left me insane.

I exist to suffer in this cosmic blaze,
the vastness by which I stand amazed.
Love casts out fear, so light my way,
a parasite, I am, at the end of the day.

Happiness is gone,
isolated again.
Love is elusive,
let's not pretend.

The High Life

Mountains line the horizon as the red moon wakes;
see the shimmering reflecting on a wave-less lake.
The breeze is soft and warm on my skin,
like the touch of a woman felt from within.
The faint scent of tulips hangs in the air,
with beauty so pure you can't help but stare.
Completely bathed in its burnished glow,
it draws you in with its magical flow.
The skies are alive the Milky Way shines bright,
to think I get to see this every night.
Now say goodbye as it takes its rest;
I'm in love with the Rockies, I do attest.

My Swan

In the sky I eye a hue of the perfect blue
like a swan in flight with beauty and power,
the graceful flew.
Following always, the need is scary;
I've lost my way.
The guardian of souls,
light to darkness, what more can I say?
You make me whole, my reason to live;
I'd give the world, if
it were mine to give.
You're the beauty to my beast,
and I'll never stray in the least.
At the slightest sight of your radiance,
my eyes get to feast.

Inhaling the Flowers

Let's spin a fantasy like an intricate web;
on the evening of life, everything's dead.
Pessimistic assumptions breeding black suspicion—
Intoxicating it is, my own intuition.
Inhaling the flames from the nefarious brood,
can you ascertain why I'm in this mood?
The wavelets of love were drawn away,
potentially causing our souls to decay.
In this pursuit of happiness, I rarely budge,
no forward momentum like it holds a grudge.
A clutched vendetta never going away—
an inconceivable price that I'm made to pay.
Explicitly barren, a decimated heart,
famished for a love that never will part.

Delusional

You call me delusional and say I'm insane;
perhaps you're right,
I must be insane to live with
the pain of your lies each night—
delusional indeed,
to believe you could change in the name of love.
Compassion, a trait you've failed to embrace,
and it was sent from above?
On this path I walk alone, and I always have;
it's no surprise my insignia in life is
a broken heart behind silent cries.
So I open my soul and the pain pours out;
the wariness drains—
a swaggering arrogance tainting the love
and leaving its stains.

Freeze the Fires

Shimmering in the darkness is how I dwell,
with a heart cold enough to freeze
the fires of Hell.

Clouded memories expelled in exchange for the clear,
endlessly roaming and
savoring the fear.

But I cannot tell what I do not know,
Extinguish this life
and let me go.

Or light the wick and make your throw.
The pressure is building;
it's set to blow.

Twisted with lunacy, take a tentative sip,
and subdue the mutiny
of this trip.

See the tendrils of lightning cross the sky,
and the pain of betrayal
is in my eye.

Refusing to Rest

The moon sits on the horizon like it's ready to fall;
clouds swirl in a pink morning sky,
and turtle doves call.
It's time to rest, but the moon won't go;
it stays in the sky,
putting on a show.
Throughout the day, it stays in sight,
battling the sun
and winning the fight.

Now the sun and the moon share the views,
and the man on the moon
enjoys the hues.
It's not just me we all can see,
when the sun comes up
and the moon won't flee.

Unworthy

Emerald eyes with auburn hair,
when you're around I can't help but stare.
Into the abyss you came for me,
expecting nothing but to set me free.

I'll give you more than I will myself;
I'm not being facetious and not speaking of wealth.
You deserve the world, if it were mine to give;
I'm on borrowed time, to love is to live.

So take my heart, it's yours to have;
walk by my side down this path.

Lays Claim

My princess is a queen, and
my queen lays claim to my heart;
for her I'd move mountains
and tear the world apart.

She gave my life purpose,
I now have a reason;
I'm no longer on the hunt,
Love's out of season.

Life isn't over ,
it's only just started;
no longer living in hell,
I've finally departed.

She's exquisitely beautiful,
and demands respect;
I'll dole out a hailstorm of pain
in order to protect.

Like a moth to a flame,
I'll burn in the fire;
unconditional love,
she's my hearts desire.

Feed the Soul

Biting your hips while gripping your thighs,
pussy dripping wet with pleasurable cries.
Pushing inside to make us whole,
the taste of each other feeds the soul.
Coming within while you ride,
hit from behind and from the side.
Perfectly round and full of flavor,
my seed you crave, and every drop you savor.
Your lollipop in life, I'll be your sucker,
but change up again and you're a dead motherfucker.
Remember my stroke and the rise of my veins;
the depths that I reach bring acceptable pains.

Never a Child

A man stands before you ,
who was never a child;
from me time was stolen,
love eclipsed by the wild.
My struggle for happiness,
a personal odyssey, what a quest;
myself my companion,
appreciated by none failing their test.
If I knew then what I know now
where would I be?
With a provocative smirk,
from the snapshots of hell setting me free?
The immensity of which
all that I've lost,
my childhood taken,
my soul was the cost.

Magical Daze

If you've wondered why I don't mention
your mind when I speak of you,
it's because deep inside you're black as night,
a hideous hue.
I admit the oversight
but enjoyed the lust,
with a magical daze.
There's something to be said about
your past and
your scandalous ways.
However, without you
I wouldn't be me,
so thank you, I will.
But don't get me wrong,
those memories of you
I still have to kill.

All My Love

Daddy's girl with bright blue eyes
That light up my world like fireworks in the skies.
Every day I fall in love with you, this is true;
it takes but a thought to warm my heart
when it comes to you.
All my love is with you all the time— have no fear—
in a perfect world
with a thousand kisses and never a tear.
My heart is alive because of your love, no doubt.
Mysteries know no limits, love prevails—let it shout.
So treasure the warmth of my words, as they are true:
you need not be sad—
Daddy's coming home to be with you.

Luring Passion

All the crazy things we've been through,
the rabble I reside with has no clue.
Of what it's like to be loved by you,
I go back in time as if I flew.
They say I'm wrong and I'm heartless,
But you see the equality of love that I bring.
But somewhere my heart turned cold,
And my anger wouldn't let me feel for a stranger.
Her luring passion infected my heart;
Immune no more, it tears me apart.
Slyly evading my questions asked,
Deceit is the culprit, and it is professionally masked.

No Rest

A dirty white boy spouting derisive laughter,
turning the pages of life starting the next chapter.
Witheringly sarcastic, arrogant at best;
if there's one thing that's promised ,
the wicked get no rest.

Dignified, yet vulgar, and perceptive to pain,
with unabashed love what a toxic stain.
The hazards in this life are tangible and real,
emanating from the shadows,
looking for souls to steal.

So let's stop the charades,
and the melodious lies.
When you smell the brimstone,
you'll make the ties.

Poetically Slain

Love what is and not what may be;
poeticize my life and set this convict free.
Perceptive to little, yet grasping for all,
inadvertently assassinated from a lover's call.

This contradiction of which I speak,
emphatically phrased and far from weak—
This slight extension of my soul,
pulls me down inside the hole.

This slight extension of my soul
pulls me down inside the hole.
Poetically slain, lies my heart;
escaping sorrow was the goal from the start.

So pacify my mind when all is going fine;
look into the mud,
because even in the dirt,
I shine.

My Pearl in Life

You are my rose and I your stem,
without the other life grows dim.
Soft candlelight on beautifully warm
skin, a sight so profound I can't
comprehend.

Reflections from your eyes keep out
the dark, that flash of radiance
melts my heart.
The thorns removed by your hands,
you're my pearl in life beneath the sands.

Sacrifices we make cause some
pain, but when made for love it's not
in vain.
I see who I want her light burns
bright, and I'll go home to you every night.

Like heaven to earth and dark to
light, my dreams come true night
after night. The love we share so
enticing and free, I offer my everything
on bended knee.

Hunger Pains

When you chew Tums at night to stop the pain,
your mind occupies a slight disdain.

The demeanor and lies you said to be slain,
a bloodless butcher's reputation in bane.

Now tendons and veins bulge and rip,
recounting the deviousness of your quip.

So as I wash the floors with my rag,
see the vacating smile begin to sag.

Hence the spite in my hiss,
there's no redemption in your kiss.

A servant of love, I was meant to be,
but only to the specter of your entity.

With the crude delight in which you take,
My protesting heart contrives to break.

Greener Grasses

For the high I chase for just a taste,
it's the feeling of love, but
to the mind it lays waste.

I'm describing a beauty that only I can see,
but this love in my life—
can I set you free?

If you seek protection from life's betrayals,
this is a guardian
that never fails.

There's always something to be done with its helping hand;
without its presence
life is bland.

The grass is greener on the other side,
so pick a vein
and enjoy the ride.

Birds of Prey

Rejoice at the sight of karma and enjoy the show;
your presumptions and betrayals will never let you go.
A loyalty unprecedented is one of might;
sticks and stones are usually what caused the fight.

But the rat's a rat to birds of prey;
you've made your bed, it's with a snitch you lay.
We work with what we have at the end of the day.
Remember I never gave up; you walked away.

So on a summer's day behind a billowy oak,
My love and I will let the sun soak.

Passion Grips

Toes digging into white sand,
a corona with lime in my hand.
I'm happy, if for the day,
as this is a time for grown-ups to play.

Rueful smiles predictably sought,
time is of the essence and love can't be bought.
A perfect fit to a deadly game,
it's the beast of love we try to tame.

So intense is the emotion when passion grips,
the hunger is wild for ruby-red lips.
But words send a chill through the soul;
everybody goes home, and once again there's a hole.

The Shepherd

I'm a wolf among sheep and playing for keeps;
I thirst for your love like a baby a teat.

I'll lie in wait as I'm forced to do,
all the while dreaming of you.

We've fought so hard and loved so deep—
can you not feel me when you sleep?

Your silken soft skin under my touch,
that look in your eyes, I miss so much.

Even though I'm gone, I'm going nowhere.
Feel my lips on your cheek, my hand in your hair.

My breath on your neck as I nibble and play—
my heart is yours and will never stray.

Your smile, your laugh, everything you do;
you stole my heart, this is true.

So hold me down the way you do,
and show me the love I never knew.

So as the days turn to night, I'll have no fear;
your love keeps me warm, your heart is near.

Karma Calls

The queen of hearts and king of spades,
ahead of the game, no matter the play.
Try and try, but can't delay
the sands of time, to their dismay.
When it comes—I mean the day—
there's not a word they will say.
Just like the wolves kept at bay,
shepherd to flock, birds of prey.
I won't lie down, not today;
I'd rather die than pave the way.
So let it rain sheets of grey,
thunder leading lightning's way.
Just like the Vikings known to slay,
when Karma calls, they shall pay.
Blood, sweat, and tears mixed with clay,
I've paid my debts day by day.

Misery Calls

It's the blue of your eyes that mesmerize,
but the sound of your voice can't disguise.
The things you hide when telling lies—
more and more, this love dies.
I'm forgetting everything, except for you;
with wretched weariness I get the clue.
Emotionally secluded, an oblivious mist,
a sadness so bleak from loved ones missed.
The skies open up and rain down pain;
end my suffering in this game.
I remember faint impressions,
waves of sadness and brutal depression.
When darkness swallows the world from within,
I'll see that faint pale glow of white skin.
When all is lifeless, a colorless grey,
misery calls love gone astray.

The Rotting

With a swirling of color and light,
a moan of death haunts this night.
By the wicked and morbid thoughts in twilight,
it feeds the pale moon shining at midnight.
My explosion of fear grips my chest,
the storms of emotions laid to rest.
With teeth that glow a greenish hue,
Phantoms banished the rotting few.
Melded sorrow with a slice of pain,
the bestial screams they cannot tame.
Purplish blues in darkening skies,
icy dews shot from fiery eyes.
Destined to live in a place of nightmares,
with the writhing monsters and lunacy shared.
My heart consumed, escapes and leaves,
like the gurgle of madness made only to flee.
The hate once seen within my eyes
was the seamstress of pain and my demise.

Honey Bee!

I'd rather walk with you in the dark
than alone in the light,
my ride, or die in this life,
and for you I'll fight.
Ups and downs
wrong or right—
what's the issue?
What's the plight?
I love you more
and more each night.
I think I may, I think I might
joke too much,
but honestly,
you're the queen of my life, my honey bee.
So walk with me
down this path;
my heart is given, it's yours to have.
Sometimes it's dark,
this is true,
but the beacon of love shines from you.

Life's Race

My life spent looking for my place,
little did I know it was in front of my face.
Modicums of compassion often come laced;
understand where you're going and give up the race.
Sculpted in stone, never to die;
I'm done looking for love, but is it done with I?
My heart was broken, but that wasn't enough;
it's my soul that was sought, wishing to snuff.
In the darkest of times you hid from the light,
so insidious you were, fueling the fight.
Love is an action, but it's also free;
I just can't understand why it eludes me.

Let Me

Let me be your best friend and lover,
your protector in life—you'll never need another.
Let me stare at you endlessly throughout the day,
and recall all the times I've had my way.
Let me take your breath one more time—
you know what I mean: your lips on mine.
Let me hold your hand in the streets
and show you off to people that we meet.
Let me breathe you in every time
I hold you gently from behind.
Let me hear you whisper that loving tune;
my heart is yours to the moon.
So goodnight, my dear, I hope it's clear:
you are my queen, never fear.

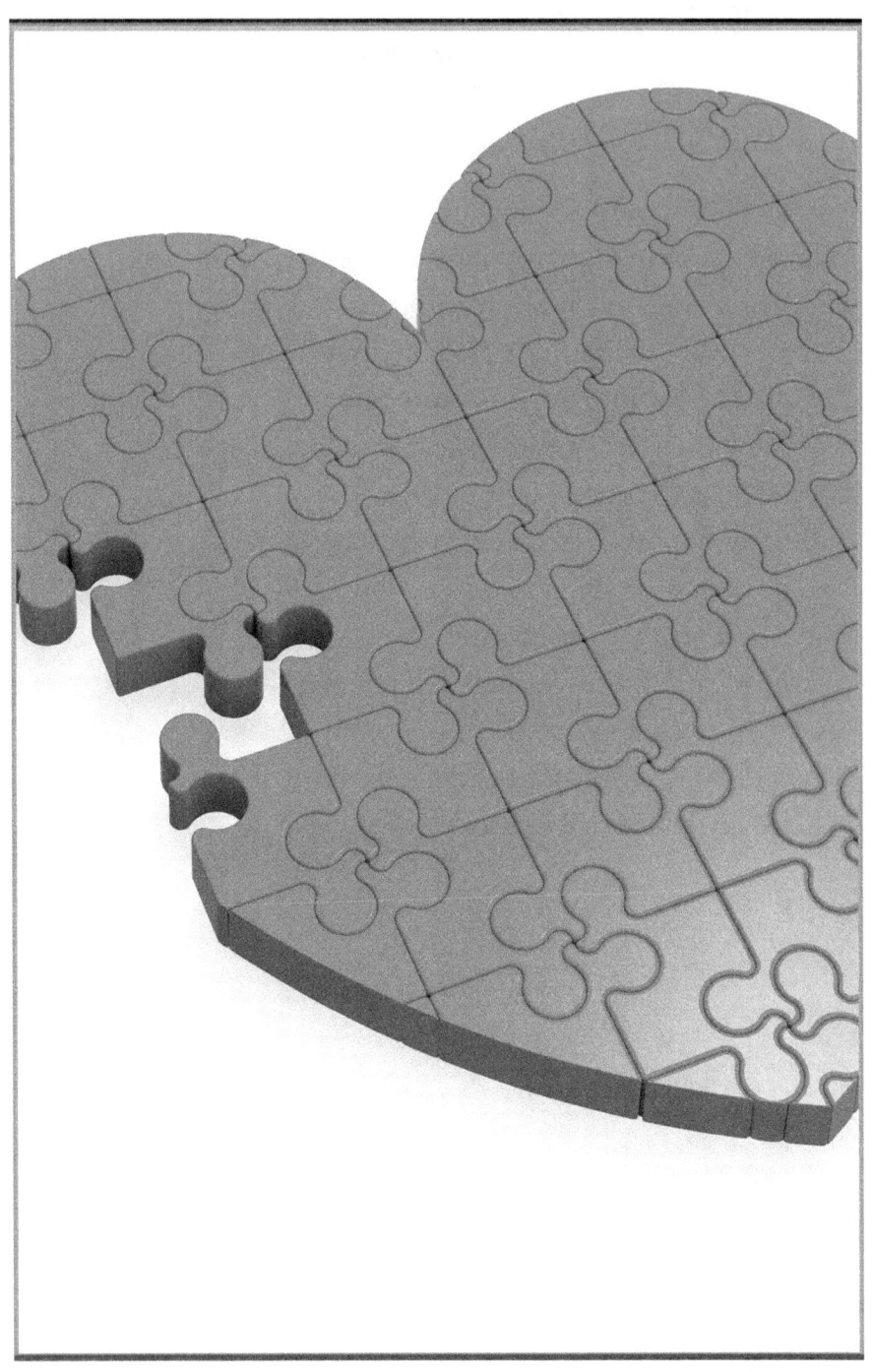

Heart's Desire

All I'll ever ask is for your love,
and I need you to know I place no one above.
I'll no longer live without passion and fire;
I'll follow my dreams and heart's desire.
Your sweet, gentle touch, I miss and crave;
without your presence my mind's dismayed.
I've not made it easy, and damn sure not free,
but the love I offer is unconditionally.
I have lied, I have stolen—this much is true—
but here are the things I'd never do:
I would not cheat your loving heart;
to do so would only tear my world apart.
So please listen as I speak the truth,
you're all that I want, love, undeniably you.
In this game of life, this puzzle we live,
you're my bordering pieces, the outline you give.

Twists and Turns

My heart's been locked, closed off from pain;
I've heard the murmurs that I'm insane.
Though not a hand, did I see,
no help offered, although I plea
until the day I met my queen,
sweet as honey and hot as steam.
Now all I want is to be free,
from the chains imprisoning me.
Bound no more, how can this be,
within four walls still is me.
It's your love that let me be,
the man before you, can't you see?
Along with happiness, I'm blissfully high
on life so mystically.
And though it's been deep within
myself all along, it seemed a sin.
To hear the tunes of laughter and love,
sent from the heavens and angels above.
So even though this road we walk
has twists and turns, do no balk.
At the bumps and hills that we pass,
this is a love made to last.

Sweet Delicacies

Wet and soft, you quiver beneath my tongue,
your intimate taste and whisperless pleas
as you come undone.

Lips tingle from the kisses I've claimed;
I'm nostalgic for passion and
a love that's untamed.

In this umbrella of love ,provoking squeals of delight,
seduction is personified by
making love in moonlight.

A sweet delicacy, you are enticing my heart,
still lured by your fragrance that I've
loved from the start.

Withered Passion

The waves recede just like your love, drawn away;
my naked hunger from starvation, as if you're my prey.
I'm at your service in solemn silence until you say
our passion has withered and you've gone astray.
With an ashen face and tears falling like rain,
the beauty of a thunderstorm has laid its claim.
Its devastating force ails my heart, neglecting my soul,
eternally forlorn, inflicted by pain, it leaves a hole.
By the animated melodramatic games you play,
from the malicious destruction perpetrated, you can smell the decay.
It's time to stop this egotistical masquerade,
so let me reiterate this cantankerous mood needs to be slain.
So fly close to the sun, but watch your wings on the way,
but remember this is the bed that you made; it's where you've lain.

Sweet Cyanide

Sleep is where your ghost lives
in the shadows of light;
condemned and tormented,
I surrender the fight.
A redheaded goddess with a taste for power,
misunderstood and plagued
by a heart turned sour.
A diversion from heartache,
and the song of pain,
dripping compassion,
with alleviating rain.
Sweet as cyanide, those moments in time—
so find love where you can;
to cheat yourself is a crime.

Nirvana Gone

It can take away your heart and murder your soul,
emotionally intimate, leaving a hole.
Exploiting the tenderness of the crass,
the nirvana they held shattered like glass.
In the midst of disaster, we can thrive,
a slave no more, I am alive.
Adored and abhorred at the same time,
your dignity's gone, the legacy's mine.
But when all it does is rain, how can I maintain?
The drops feel like acid eating my brain,
these exotic spasms lethally felt,
with daggers of lightning cleverly dealt.
So save yourself and run away,
before you're infected and made to pay.

Love Softly

More compassion than most, yet loved by few,
the one that does was right on cue.
My mind races when you're not near,
and the sound of your voice, I need to hear.
I dream of your beauty and perfect smile;
you surpass them all in a country mile.
Descend from heaven on the wings of an angel,
love me softly, and please don't mangle.
What we share in the meadows of love
must have been sent down from above.
So fill my sails full with gales,
the breath of the gods, a long exhale.

Drink You Up

From the moment I saw you, I knew I must
roll the dice of love—it's all or bust.
It cannot tarnish and does not rust,
but will turn you red and make you blush.

I'd sip your tears and swallow your pain,
even if it means going insane.
Let love run free and dance in the rain,
while my eyes drink you up like sweet champagne.

The dust of a backroad driven at dusk,
the twinkle in your eye betrays your lust.
The love I found is profound;
once in a lifetime it comes around.

Just like my heart from the start,
it's in your hands to tear apart.
My world, my life is in vain;
to go away would leave me slain.

I may be gone, but I like the song,
I'm still right there—
this won't last long.

Feed the Hunger

So this is what's done when a man tries to change:
everybody runs.
No more support, morale, or money—and then wonder why
I look at them funny.
Not really knowing what this creates,
but I tell you now it's bred from hate.
But to feed the hunger, one must do the vilest things and
prey on you.
The sad thing is, this is true:
I'll do what I must, this you knew.
I'm on the hunt, so the weak beware:
I'll take what I want without a care.

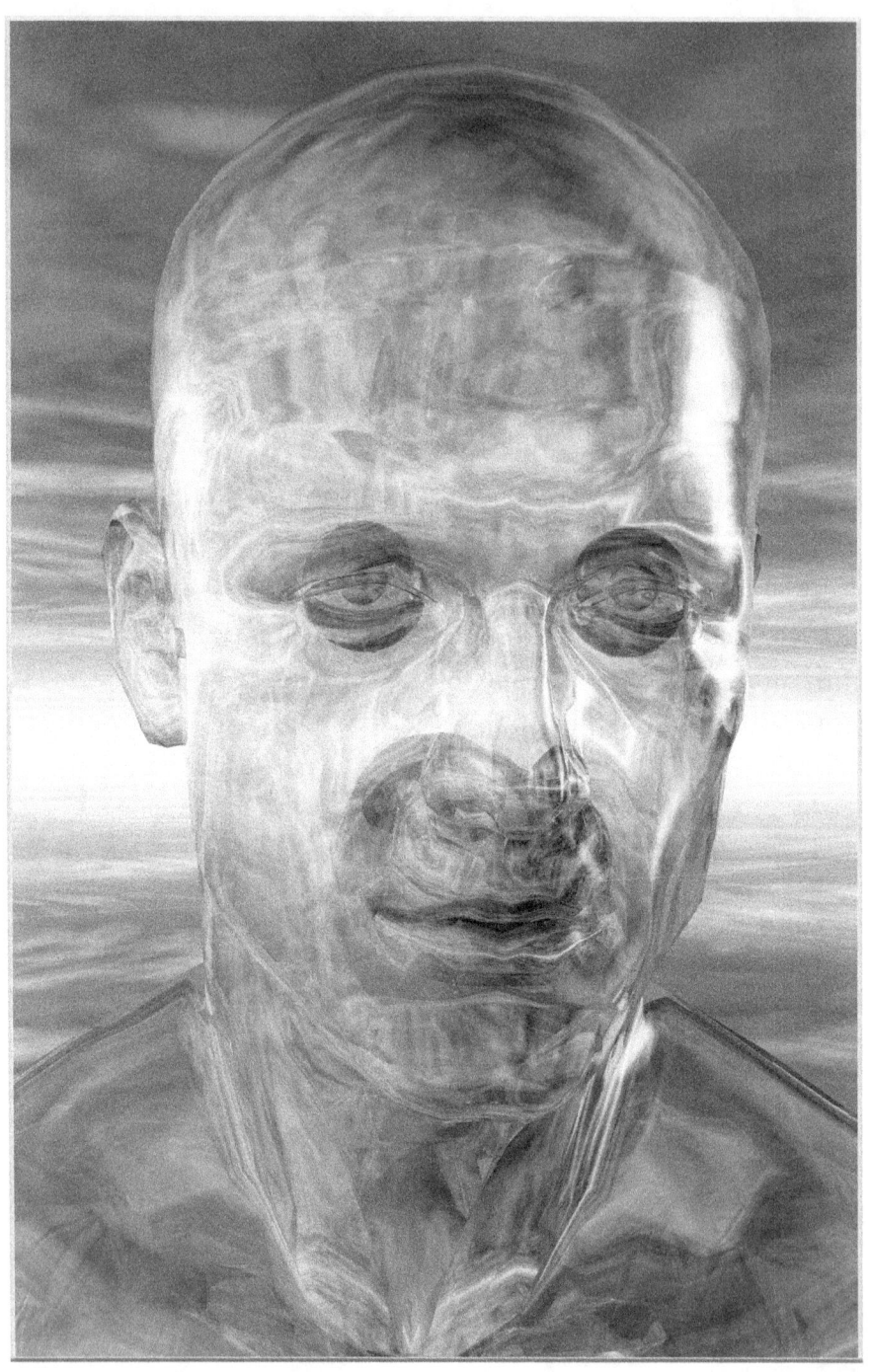

Mr. Misunderstood

Perception of a man that you cannot see
although he stands in the light,
shoulders sagging in his shadow as if
he lost the fight.
Little do you know the good which he's done;
you focus on the stains
from the mud in which he's run.
Often misunderstood
and constantly confused,
he's tired of a broken heart
and always being used.
So do not judge the book until you've read the last word;
believe half of what you see,
and none of what you've heard.

Abandon My Heart

Understand me when I fail, and hold me in the rain,
I'm not the best of men;
I'm guilty of causing pain.
I'm empty in every way since you abandoned my heart;
your love seems foreign,
receding and ready to depart.
Your presence is profound and sprouted from last;
once you get a taste,
she becomes a must.
An invasion of the soul, extinguishing the mind,
a pitiful confinement—
the manipulating kind!

Limits of Love

Behind these bars I'm stuck in time,
yet told by you your heart's still mine.
The length I face can decline
the love we share—is it blind?
As hard as I try, I can't define,
the same I feel when looking behind.
It kills me over and over again
to know it was me who went within
the limits of love, yet did not sin.
Yes, I'm a mess, but doing my best
to be deserving of you,
I must confess.
I'm a humble man who may be damned;
at your mercy, I cannot stand.
Now I kneel as should be,
expressing myself down on one knee.
So what do you say, what will it be?
Leave me lonely or marry me.

Paid in Flesh

A wasted moon fails to rise,
I fall to the dirt, yet kiss the sky.
The price of betrayal paid in flesh,
hear the earth draw in its breath.
Eyes brighter than precious gems,
stars twinkle out death from within.
So fathom the thoughts and words I speak;
yes, it's me, just no longer meek.
Half-rotted hearts, ghost of a breeze,
has plagued my past and fed my disease.
In a prison of pain, screams of madness,
the monarch of demons will relish sadness.
Now I'm battle-hardened, tattooed, and scared,
but never again caught off-guard.

Turned Black

The soulless stand, dazed and in a haze,
living in the past, stuck in the maze.
A palpable sadness continues to grow,
just like your heart, cold as snow.
Walk on in, you can feel the despair,
paranoia sparked like a lightning flare.

You cannot see the world's turned black,
jaded and broken from the attack.
Impulsive and reckless, the mind shies away;
by numbing the veins,
pain's kept at bay.

My Redemption

I've been tried in the fires of life,
and it's all or nothing;
with social sanity lost,
there's no time for bluffing.

Flowing from my soul,
I've lost my way;
faith is my redemption
I'll willingly pay.

In a crisis, I lived,
brought it on myself;
the curtain has closed,
I'm on the shelf.

But he was there
when no one else'd seen
that I needed it most,
and he let me lean.

So love the light
and walk inside;
don't be ashamed,
no need to hide.

Hands of Time

The sands erode just like the mind;
we are all of us racing the hands of time.
Like a light brush of fingers across my mind,
my memory plays tricks, exciting the blind,
mutually silent while humoring the kind,
accusingly ashamed because there's nothing to find.
The eruption of panic starts to bind,
conveniently hindering while tearing the rind.
The formalities over on the line you signed;
sanity's lost—better yet, left behind.

Voices of Silk

With cat-like eyes and a smile of seduction,
she grips your soul;
basking in her beauty in a trance-like state,
your heart is stole.
Now sit and wait on the bench
of fate as the times pass,
counting the grains as the sands
fall through the hourglass.
Her voice of silk
ties you up and won't let go;
there's no need to fight—
you cannot win and won't say no.
So pledge your love
and devote your life before it's taken away;
make her your queen—
make her your wife and
beg her to stay.

Compelled

Smiles vanish in the countenance
of evil, feel the twinges of pain.
Overly unique,
the end of a soul, you can sense the insane.
Brilliant green eyes compel you within,
infused with sorrow and a hint of sin.
It is concealment of rage,
but the hatred shows,
ashamed from guilt that nobody knows—
blinding agony,
inflicting revenge you refused to see.
That vengeance is mine;
I've come to reclaim what's been taken from me.

Follow My Gaze

The inanity of life and the emptiness that is you,
I grasp for your heart to end our despair,
but it grew wings and flew.
Leached off your soul,
its deadness you carry
like clouds to rain.
In a sky tinged with purple, follow my gaze,
mistress of pain seeking revenge,
licking your tears.
So I'll sing my song with you in mind as I'm on my way,
Like your heart the world grows cold
day after day.

Shooting Stars

Baby blues like faded Levis,
lightning bugs in the summer skies.
Slow dancing under shooting stars,
to the moon and back or maybe Mars.
I'll walk from nowhere to pointlessness,
all for the softness of your kiss.
Hues of dawn, it's inviting light,
with peaks of mountains in all their might.
Your love melted my heart with a gaze;
like the flames of Hell, this fire's ablaze
from the harmony heard in your words,
like waking to the sound of birds.
With a glimpse of perfection you become an obsession;
from the rooftops hear my painful inflection.
I'll always see you and remember the smile
that melted my heart, there is no denial.

Metaphors of Love

The specter of death herself in demonic clarity haunts my dreams,
I run and I hide, but she's always there getting closer, it seems.
The paradox is: she has a warm light and delicate touch;
It's comfort during the death of my faith, not that I ever had much.
She quiets the tide of emotion flooding my brain;
from a slithering tongue that hisses lies, I've gone insane.
Keep your head up, is what I'm told; nothing good comes from the ground except flowers,
but even those will waste your time if you count the hours.
There's a golden rule I must convey:
don't give up your heart and keep her at bay.

Dripping Drool

Adequately negligent, treacherous and cruel,
gloriously deformed with saliva dripping drool.
Feel the rending of flesh as it's torn away;
your temerity is broken as blood starts to spray.
Brandishing disregard for the desecrated souls,
strangling the entities ideally filling holes.
Predictability intrigued by the ritual and rites,
Poison-covered fangs deeply feeling bites.
Like a gargoyle's shadow cast by the moon,
the malignant concerns dictating your doom.
Your integrity's lost to the contemptuous deceiver,
indicating you're a hostage, some call you a believer.

Never Fair

Sometimes I sit and wonder how my heart
has gone a-plunder;
poetically I am dead,
body and soul have gone asunder.

I summon up the strength not to act
before I think;
courage comes with knowledge
when disaster is on the brink.

Despair is in the air and
love is never fair;
it dies each time it lands on me,
and nobody seems to care.

With a past I don't condone,
my future has been shown:
misery, pain, and heartache—
alone, I hold the throne.

Angela Lynn

As you sit upon a throne of pleasure,
I am your humble servant.
With the pearl of love on my tongue,
you'd think I was a serpent.

I smile inwards as you descend
deeper into orgasmic bliss,
begging me to stop
while you continue to mist.

Things amplify when I indulge
with the tip of my love;
I'm not ravaging your body
that fits like a glove.

A cosmic explosion
bursts from within,
suffused with a feeling
we can't comprehend

I deliberately go
where no other's gone before,
dedicated to your pleasure
in which you implore.

It's coming to an end,
my climax in sight;
I'll grab your throat and smack your ass,
as if in a fight.

It's nearly over, as I beg *don't stop,*
come again,
all the while saying your name:
Angela Lynn.

Heated Kisses

With pearlescent skin and a
hint of lavender on the air,
lips heated with swollen kisses,
this just isn't fair.

That soft sound that
escapes your throat,
I offer you pleasure.
Will you hit the note?

A woman of vitality,
your aura shines through,
flowing from your pores,
blinding me—it's true.

Ineptitude at romance,
we can finally see;
it's sculpted from the heavens,
you are meant for me.

The melodramatic dialogue
in which I say it loud;
screaming from the rooftops,
see me standing proud.

I pray this makes an impact—
my theory is it might—
the woman that I dream of,
I have her in my sight . . .

Paranoia

Tatted like a biker and ready for war,
Paranoia, my friend, knowing what's in store,
stalking my prey with malevolent might,
the inevitable outcome blinded in fright.

Grimacing pain that can't be ignored
from the incendiary fires of the dark lord,
your composure crumbles when you hear the sound
from the gleaming claws that tap the ground.

The unfamiliar presence of the insidious man
inhabiting your nightmares, not knowing the plan;
from out of the shadows this figure loomed
with escalating madness, you know you're doomed.

A freakish savage,
a paragon from hell;
get ready for vengeance,
ready to quell!

Tethered to Sanity

I've seen you bathed in moonlight—a divine love story
like the golden gleam of a halo, in all its glory—
but as I sit and do my time, I can't help but wonder
if your heart is really mine, or did someone plunder?

It would leave me empty, like a vast void.
I'm in the abyss you all but destroyed;
it's true, everybody gets burned, when it comes to the flame,
but you wouldn't feel so good, if it weren't for pain.

Have mercy on this man and bring him back to the fold,
as somewhere down the line, my heart turned cold;
inevitably transformed and tethered to sanity
the friend of silence screams life's profanity.

Death must be simple, as living is hard,
battle-tested and proven, visibly scarred;
in the dirt, I'm found, but shine I do.
I'm a diamond in the rough; I thought you knew.

A king in life,
yet I am meek;
it's the crown of love
I do seek.

My Cameo

As the tide breaks on the sand
I look in your eyes and take your hand;
my cameo or perhaps my breath,
to be without you means my death.

A hint of perfection intertwined in bliss,
the victorious feeling of a seductive kiss,
it's that floral scent that fills the air;
find me lingering without a care.

Your curvaceous body in a shimmery sheen—
the temptation's deliberate; you made it be seen
with love declared; I'll fondle your heart,
affirming those thoughts you had from the start.

Slumbering King

In the void I live, a downpour of mystery—the seed of revenge, a tide of misery. Numb and withered this deadening pain, the crown of chaos on the slumbering king. Unearthly anguish from acid in my veins; delirious mourning, the reckoning came.

Dreary days lit with lunacy and regret, bloodshot eyes from festering madness, I came here to forget.
Engulfed by malice and mirrored by nothingness, entombed by the underworld in absolute darkness. Indistinct drumming, rejoice if you can; the slumbering king wakes and walks among man.

Disgusted Desire

A hushed awe falls over the crowd;
the numbness in common
is like the shroud.

This ancient flame, a searing heat,
dominated the plane's and
took his seat.

The shame inflicted and trapped inside,
this horrendous cycle
you cannot hide.

Lances of pain—an agonizing shiver,
disgusted desire makes
you quiver.

So compose yourself as you see the sickle,
igniting the creepiness,
luring the fickle.

Wince, you will, and squeal, you might;
he's harshly collecting his
dues this night.

Crave!

Forged in the fires of love,
she was my soul;
cupping her face while kissing those lips,
with hooded eyes, my heart she stole.

Absorb the taste that's been buried in her,
flooding the heart,
a need to devour the magically magnificent,
but worlds apart.

Blissfully ignorant while I dine on her skin—
too precious a sight—
memories of you swim through my mind;
I give up the fight.

I crave your warmth and drown in need,
such a fragile shell;
the thoughts of possibilities tears at my heart
as I bid you farewell.

To Behold

Everything about you is
Temptation, and my defenses crumble.
Loving you terrifies me,
yet here I stand, humble.

The way your hand held
mine on a moonlit night;
the most beautiful to behold,
in the pale shimmering light.

You bring me comfort
when all is lost.
This love, I long to return to you,
no matter the cost.

So pursue you, I will,
until death tears us apart.
It is no lie that you
captured my heart.

War of Words

It's a war of words within my head.
Rotten to the core, I must be dead.
But in death I fly like a bird,
so grab a dictionary to learn the word.

It's never gonna stop, so rest assured,
I'm a lyrical trigger killing the verb.
I know you're thinking this is absurd,
But I'm at the top of my game and must be heard.

So the conclusion is this,
do not miss,
because life or limb
I take the risk.

And with potent vernacular
rarely seen,
bow your head—
I am the king!

Razor's Edge

On the razor's edge of madness,
sanity gleams brightly, slipping down
below, falling further nightly.
Nerves of steel to a rational
thought, transfixed in fear with
bravery naught.
From the maniac's chuckle to his
bulging eyes,
in his hollow gaze feel your demise.
With boldness gone you're
whisked away,
on a raging river of hate, you shall stay.
Infected with doubt, blindly shaking,
from a crippling roar
feel the awakening.
The unbearable guilt lances your heart,
while the shine of the
blade takes its part.

Cusp of Heaven

Roses bloom forever, and we will part no more,
concentrating on this romance and what's in store.
We've lived a crazy life, so let's make things right,
kissing velvety soft lips in the glow of northern lights.
I am your man among men, and I'm under your spell;
we're on the cusp of heaven—it's obtainable, you can tell.
I'd move the stars by hand to write you a love note;
I am your alpha and omega—not trying to gloat.
My breath on your skin sends chills to your core,
reverberating my love for you like waves on a shore.

Life's Endeavour

The taste of your kiss soaked in wine,
with the sun sinking down from behind.
Remember when I filled you with
excruciating pleasure, seductive and
sensual, my life's endeavor?
Seeing you smile pales to your laugh—
my love, I give, it's yours to have.
Feel my hands tangle in your hair,
my lips on your neck, nibbling with care.
You may not believe, but I tell it true,
my heart of hearts belongs to you.
Try, they may, to come between,
a love like ours has been foreseen.
I can't give in or be the one
to break your heart and make you run.
In my arms warm and safe,
Angel-soft, amazing grace.
I never imagined the storms we weathered;
a love like this lasts forever.

War Wounds of Love

Deeply entrenched, conflicted and torn,
stolen memories—a concept
you can't help but mourn.

The slickness of sweat,
intrusive but real,
like the war wounds of love you nauseously feel.

The commitment seems meek and
appallingly weak; with composure
regained, its mercy I seek.

And pursue with strained courage
resisting the fear,
sacrificing my pride and making it clear.

To salvage this love from
sorrow and pain,
I've battled insanity, leaving it slain.

So let me cuddle your heart and
cradle your soul;
I've told you before, I'll never let go!

Extravagant Views

Two stars, light years away,
Twinkling bright wanting to play.
Extravagant views in so many hues,
A rainbow during sunset let go of the blues.

Smile and let the warmth shine,
An amazing sight sending shivers down my spine.
Fondling my heart and inhaling my love,
Our souls entwined, fitting like a glove.

Abstract as quizzical art,
Never could I imagine being apart.
An intoxicating scent borne on the breeze,
Never let down, you always please.

Velvet lips like an angel's kiss,
There's not a second I'd agree to ever miss.
I feel your embrace and hold it dear,
Reminiscing everything and keeping it clear.

Love Flows

With a love as pure as freshly fallen snow;

and as ancient as the temples where the Mayans

used to go,

My colorful command of language, subtle and unique,

but the way in which my love flows can never be oblique.

The audacity in which you gave my heart the boot,

gives the impression your feelings were always moot.

I'm fascinated by your charm and how you kept me hooked;

your dereliction is profound—you came for what you took,

leaving me distraught, indignant to the pain

entirely; I've gone utterly insane.

I Am Bane

In a battle of wits, I'm a verbal assassin;

while they're standing still, I blow right past 'em.

Pullin' the trigger with these words,

killin' the nouns and slayin' the verbs.

In this realm I am Bane,

I took the crown, it's mine to claim.

So before you go against the king, remember

that this monarch wears the ring.

I set the pace for you to follow;

good luck with this pill, it's hard to swallow.

So take a drink; I think you're choking

from what I said, but I'm not joking.

Don't feel sad, or ashamed.

Lick your wounds; you've been maimed.

Unbound by Man

You're my inspiration, this is true.

Flood gates have opened, you have no clue.

What you're capable of, you do not see,

and no, I don't mean figuratively.

Build me up or tear me down,

a blind man walking to lead me now.

To your lane of love, you wear the crown,

the palace of hearts, I follow the sound.

Covered in roses, your soft velvet skin,

seems like eternity, not being within.

Your garden of love, let's not pretend,

what my touch can do, no others can.

So feel your cheek within my hand,

the warmth we share like sun to sand.

Like riverlets of water together expand,

our love unbridled and unbound by man.

She Peeks

Wrapped around her pinky,
A fool for her, I be.
With smiling eyes and a satiny voice,
a princess she is to me.

Innocent and pure,
amiably she speaks.
Snuggled with me when it's time for bed,
through hooded eyes, she peeks.

We would dance in the kitchen
and hold each other tight.
She's a queen among angels;
in the darkness, she is light.

Just to watch her sleep,
I was lucky to see.
I failed to state her name,
But clearly it's Riley!

Preludes to Love

My mind wanders in a Nirvana's mist;

velvety soft is your dainty kiss.

Lavender scrim in a softening sky,

wind chimes twinkle, a breeze passed by.

Seen from high terraces, beauty rules,

mitigated by nothing, my love pools.

That rippling infectious giggle

Makes my heart soar;

perpetually obsessed, I shamelessly adore.

And I indefinitely admire the elegance in which

your beauty keeps me frozen; in my heart

I feel the stitch.

Presumably regal, and I call you my queen,

the prelude is over; we've outlived the obscene.

Death Wish

In a cell is where I dwell,

with the smell of despair.

"Welcome to Hell."

My death wish remains unanswered,

and I don't know why;

On an endless sea of torment

I hang my head and cry.

This insurmountable urge

to pull the trigger on Life,

halitosis of the soul

smothered in strife.

So until Death calls for me,

it's revenge I seek.

My heart has been callused

and is no longer weak.

The Squeal

Feathery soft kisses from you, I miss;

getting drunk on your taste is utter

bliss.

I can't explain how I've become so fond;

my capacity for forgiveness speaks of our

bond.

Those baby-blue, half-hooded eyes,

that seductive giggle while I'm kissing

your thighs.

My tongue explores all your curves

and dips that squeal of pleasure when

I nibble your hips.

Lightly licking and caressing your pearl,

I pick up the pace and your toes curl.

Scream my name and dig at my back; the

beast of your beauty—that's just a snack!

Walled Away

Revenge is my mistress, and inflicting pain

is her goal;

with the hint of a smile and a gleam in her

eye, she will take your soul.

The embarkation of misery in her perfunctory way,

inhaling her aroma while begging her to stay.

Anger creates destruction that's walled away

from trust; the sense of distance from your soul

doesn't compare to the lust.

So prattle about as she strips you to the bone,

her smile is false; she holds no love, this

she has shown.

Black as death is her heart—just look inside;

run if you can and lock the doors—she's coming,

so hide!

Savage Grin

Within the lion's lair, I've lain,
cast aside to the pits of hell,
I must pay.

Hideous fear from pain endured a broken soul;
the lore and gore from warped minds has
taken its toll.

Incomplete and damaged, the pain is mine along with madness;
the constraints of compassion no longer hold
the certainty of sadness.

Falling deeper into a sea of despair with a savage grin,
squeals of rage; a shrieking litany is
born of sin.

His lips are twisted to a sinister smirk,
morbidly looking with bloodshot eyes and
a sardonic quirk.

The Brink

For a glimpse into hell, just
follow me down a spiral of
insanity to an ominous sea.

See the harsh stare from the
mask of misery, or fickle
smirk given so vividly,

Where the eerie silence is
broken by a gurgling scream, and
the haunted souls provide a ghastly gleam.

See the fear frozen in a
hideous scowl; welcome to Hell—
some call it the bowel.

Vicious obscenities from a
demonic beast, covered in
blood from its sadistic feast.

With oblivion seen in just a
wink, let's all go swan dive
past the brink.

Kissing the Sky

Losing the battle within—can someone remind me who I am? All I know is it's dark, and Hell is hot; this must be a sham.

I scream at the heavens, give me back my soul; hear my hoarse cries, I've paid the toll.

Nothing else matters but kissing the sky; with a dimly lit view, in the abyss, I lie.

I know I'm lost; there is a debt to be paid but I know not the cost.

Spilling my heart with a bloody pen, we all get dirty, even the best of men.

Magnificent Nomad

Circumventing my heart, a hasty
defection, a magnificent nomad
of love's inflection.
Cold as snow and half past
crazed, the guttural sounds
come from the haze.
A poisonous weed grows within
my brain, lashing at my will,
blocking out the pain.
See the searing agony my
eyes do hold; you can't be
saved from yourself, I'm told.
An indescribable torment humming
inside, adoringly morbid and
straining to hide.
A slave, I've become, because
I professed, a venomous touch,
A deadly caress.

Souls Sold

I sold my soul—can I buy it
Back? I'll give you twice what
you paid, even though it's black.
Fossilized and lame, it's integrity's
bost; I was given but a fraction
of its actual cost.

Pure, it's not, and through the mud
it's crawled; I've misspent my life enormously flawed.
I'm almost home—I've found my
Way; with my soul intact, I'll eagerly pay.
When I sold my soul for what I thought was a
home, I really sold my soul just to be alone.

Riley's

Blond hair and bright blue eyes,
Dad's saving grace, it's no surprise.
I remember when you first
came home, the snuggles shared,
the love that was shown.

You'd mumble these words, and it was sweet,
"My little love-bug."
Aren't you neat?
The pitter-patter of little feet,
On my chest you'd fall asleep.

I'd play with your hair every night,
until you'd snore,
eyes closed tight.
Light up my life with a laugh.
You stole my heart;
it's yours to have.

My princess, you are—and a queen,
you'll be. I know you're confused
and missing me.
These are all things that are meant to be.
Daddy's coming home,
you will see!

Free in Life

Like a sparrow in flight, it's an eye's
delight, so graceful and sleek—but
nothing compared to the mountains
in May with their snow-covered peaks.
Or how about the mist that hangs
in the air without a care, and the
shooting stars that light the sky
while you stare?

With the sun shining on the grass,
covered in dew, and the moonlight
glow surrounding your love in a
beautiful hue,
all of these things are free
in life, yet rarely seen—at least until
it's too late, it would seem.

Loyalty Over Love

Loyalty over love, it's a way of life
and how to live. I dimly remember a
reverse scenario and how I'd forgive.
I lost myself to find the man I
am today, unspeakable losses from
the sacrifices I had to pay.

I jumped in head-first despite the
signs, tiptoeing on egg shells
and side-stepping mines.
I could see the hate infusing your
soul; it consumes your life and
takes a toll

On us all, and we become deranged,
dismembering ourselves and
ignoring the strange.
Call it a malady, call me insane,
spent a life searching for love
I could never obtain.

Reign of Sorrow

My heart remains pure
in the trenches of profanity;
my mind is what's been tainted,
living with insanity.

To hell with the sentiments
from a deathly silent night,
the scraps of my soul picked clean by the vultures
too bloated to take flight.

As I shake my head,
the demons inside bounce around;
festering and raw, they scream
without making a sound.

In the swirling images of anguish,
the tsunami hits the shore;
enmeshed in toxicity,
the reign of sorrow starts to pour.

Killing My Faith

I sit and I watch and I wait my turn
for that which I seek;
if I'm laid to rest and buried deep,
let the insects creep.

But revitalize my soul after the
theft of my heart,
the architect of love—
let Cupid play his part!

The intimacy generated
a keenness for your scent;
deliriously dream-like,
our time has come and went.

Systematically killing my faith,
loyalty crafted from your lies;
no more being facetious—
the only thing left saying is "Goodbye."

Fog of Fatigue

Legitimately spontaneous and eternally hopeless—
some things just are, out of sight, out of mind,
like a cloud-covered star.

In a fog of fatigue from the darkest days,
seen—but sunshine the goal—when it rains,
it pours, explaining my reluctance to expose my soul.

As the decades pass, in my quest for love,
the intensity fades, my loyalty plots against me;
the colors are shown in all their shades.

Call me insane, but there's a place
in my brain where the treacheries end, but if I'm buried alive with
psycho lunatic neighbors, how can I mend?

Numero Uno

A galaxy of stars dims, compared to my love for you;
dancing barefoot in the moonlight while stealing a kiss,
my heart is true.

I ache for your touch and a virtuous life,
a legacy shared, charm conveyed with comparative warmth,
my feelings flared.

Engendering confidence, the energy from these striking views,
meticulously loved my *numero uno*;
you are my muse.

Under the moon and the stars on sugary sand with your lips on mine,
it's these precious little moments of expressive beauty
that make planets align.

Colors of Insanity

I'm all right, but the world's all wrong—
what can I say?
Your lies darken your heart,
exposing your soul—there's a price to pay.

My chest is hollow and void of love
from the games that you play.
I'm over my past, but is it over me
at the end of the day?

It is my burden and I will not share,
as it belongs to me.
Call me selfish, but
living eternally comes with a fee.

If you're afraid of the dark,
have no fear, just seek the light,
wait for me in the color of insanity
where the flame is bright.

Love Burns

You're gonna miss this
when I take it all away;
you'll remember all the times I showered you with love
and how I had asked you to stay.

It was the grandest of gestures,
but my composure returns, my ray of light in the darkness;
my heart's ablaze and love burns.

A heaviness has fallen, and just like that
love dies,
stridently cruel with a jadedness and
unbidden tears in your eyes.

As the gears of deceit engage
behind greenish-grey eyes,
not even the beauty you possess
will hide all your lies.

Black Roses

The windows to my soul are
guarded and barred,
anger and pain replacing compassion,
leaving my heart scarred.

Hopelessness perceived,
so let me surmise,
loyalty eludes me—
it will be my demise.

Lasting charisma,
a broken heart begs to thrive;
you are an infection,
destroying what's alive.

Impervious to compassion,
strident warnings ringing clear,
black roses laid on the grave of our love,
and you never shed a tear.

No Mercy

If you're reading this
it's too late,
so embrace the life we know;
pull up a plate.

As you peek through the keyhole
while standing in the rain,
you'll get no mercy
from the insane.

You may lose it all
before you win,
so dot your I's
in this life of sin.

The ruling king of heathens,
I have the clout;
I'll pop the top—
have no doubt.

I tie myself to loyalty
with a chain,
never receiving
anything but pain.

Money is the motive—
hear my decree—
pledge your allegiance
down on one knee.

Skinning Cats

Men all my life
have been trying to break me;
leave it to a woman to succeed.
I guess it always comes to the exposed heart
in a time of need.

You played your games
and you played them well,
leaving me alone to a life of hell.
Soon I'll be gone, I promise you that,
there's more than one way to skin a cat.

Sailing alone, tormented by the blisters you left,
my love's been pilfered, laced in pain
since the theft.
Debilitating anguish deteriorates a just soul,
limping away, licking hounds' wounds from a heart to a hole.

If I Die

Hear the hunger in my voice
when I speak of love and devotion,
but see the hesitation from fear
in feeling this emotion.

Watching from the shadows
as my momentum grows,
I can't bring back what's taken from me
or thaw a heart that's froze.

Make me an immortal
if I die tonight; remember me for eternity—
like a star
burning bright.

We are all of us perfect
to someone, somehow;
my heart beats to the tune of love—
just listen to it now.

Bullets of Sorrow

Fueled by vengeance
and draped in chains,
never free until retribution is claimed,
an external nightmare is where I live
and I cannot wake;
find me alone in the shelter of despair.
It was built by the fake.
All I had to give wasn't enough to sate your thirst,
bullets of sorrow shot from the tongue
with a deafening burst.

Succeeding, my heart is an empty shell
that craves to give,
a scant amount of the insanity
in which I live.

Cold

Look into these steel grey eyes and realize
they are as cold as your heart.
Understand the level of pain creating this distance
that has torn us apart.
Think of the sacrifices made
from all the times you wanted your way,
and ponder the years I sit wasting,
severed from everything, watching my freedom decay.
Contemplate on the hate that
you deliver like fate;
while your past makes you miserable,
my future is looking great.

Love is Bane

Home stretch of heartache,
I contemplate the bane from love;
frozen in the death of betrayal,
I go insane.

Love is pain and
loyalty is law;
it's a pragmatic gesture,
if I ever saw.

Time heals all wounds,
but a heart is not simple;
loneliness devours a soul and
can leave you a cripple.

Where there's smoke
there's bound to be fire;
with burning eyes,
start deciphering desire.

Screaming out loud,
"Death to a traitor!"
For my loved ones, I'm a gangster—
don't be a hater.

Mary Jane

The power of Mary Jane's flower—
from cotton candy to sour—
it can leave you stuck in a daze,
daydreaming of a magical tower.

It can make you sit and wonder
of the rain and sounds of thunder;
or if you shared your sack,
would your love have gone asunder.

She is sunshine in a bag,
and you will never hear her nag;
the more often you indulge,
the more likely you are to lag.

So pack up your bowl
or roll up a joint;
put a flame to Mary Jane—
I think you get the point.

Chasing the Cat

Sniffing dream dust and escaping to the bedroom,
it's time to play;
you've been a bad girl,
so with whips and chains I'll make you pay.
I drink in your scent like
a glass of wine and I think I'm drunk.
A sucker for love, always chasing the cat
like Pepe the Skunk.
I'd trade everything just to taste the curve of your hips,
or to feel the softness and velvety texture
once again of your lips.
To be blessed by the sound of your voice
tickles my heart,
and once I'm inside, you'll be screaming my name.
Are you ready to start?

Camo'd Out

I'm camo'd out like I'm in the military.
Try riding my wave;
you're left in a cemetery.

I'm a sucker for pain,
and I never stand down,
beaten like a stepchild every time you're around.

My God is my judge,
and he sees it all;
no matter the charge ,your boy stands tall.

A savage life is all I know,
in a red delago,
with money to blow.

All the chirping is for the birds—
and that's a fact—
leader of the herds, alpha of the pack.

I stand on two feet—
that's all ten toes—
play with me and nobody knows.

At the end of the day,
you'll call the police,
because when I catch you it's "Rest in Peace."

Beauty

There is beauty behind this fence
and these walls;
it's amazingly loud,
yet without a sound
destroying my calls.

In a way unknown
I'm revealed; this sight
of pink-fringed
purplish-clouds
just before the night.

The smell of sweet bush
floats on the air,
while I pick daisies
on a back road
without a care.

The beauty I speak of
is tainted by none except for peace
on a pedestal of love;
infections to all known
never to cease.

Nuances Noted

Tatted and gatted,
I'm ready for war—
do you really think
you're ready for what's in store?
Let's stir the pot
and watch it brew;
smell the aroma
of this toxic stew.

Frantically manic,
a dissenter of dictators;
if not for you, I'd never be known—
thank you, my haters.
Like bloated bodies left behind
from subsequent events,
every nuance is noted while living eccentrically—
you feel the extents.

This path I walk alone
with my head held high;
if my voice is heard, let me know
and I'll tell you why.

Play My Part

I'm 200 pounds of twisted steel.
You say you want smoke—
it's blisteringly real.

The devil's advocate, I play my part.
Revenge is my mistress—
she holds my heart.

Picasso with a pen, when I let it flow,
there's a story in my eyes—
welcome to the show.

Unapologetic allegiance, self-centered at best;
in the darkness I wander
while in the depths I rest.

Slow trickles

Drowning in the slow trickles
of anger and pain;
a brief break in the clouds is all I ask
before going insane.

Blindsided by rage,
my primal beast,
this status quo an encore of love;
I've told you before I'll never let go.

Dead and devoid of all feeling,
the release of sleep,
going to the warmth like a sparkling sun,
breathing weak.

Endurance is gone,
and life seems to wither out;
broken, this man crushed a soul—
there is no doubt.

Instincts Rot

Humanity weakens in the coils of pain;
Tears glisten, leaving their stain.

Heinous spirits resisting the light,
sullenly dull and massing to flight.

With fire in my veins, vile and hot,
a false hope lingers and instincts rot.

The bloodthirsty try to quench their thirst;
I won't be faded, as I shoot first.

Hear the slurs from the strewn who crumble;
in agonizing defeat, they frantically mumble.

A gnawing filthiness foreign and slight,
it's done on a whim and done in spite.

I'm the savior of bane and I do claim:
With an iron fist, I was born to reign.

Never Fair

Sometimes I sit and wonder
how my heart has gone a-plunder;
poetically I am dead--
body and soul have gone asunder.

I summon up the strength
not to act before I think;
courage comes with knowledge,
and disaster's on the brink.

Despair is in the air
and love is never fair;
it dies each time it lands on me,
and nobody seems to care.

With a past I don't condone,
my future has been shown:
misery, pain, and heartache—
alone, I hold the throne.

Get Dough

Stacking bread like a baker,
I'm about my cake;
eating good like health food,
it's these haters I shake.

If you haven't caught on,
I'll say it slow;
everything that I do
involves getting dough.

From counting my cheese—
you know I mean cheddar—
it's racks on racks,
you'll never do better.

The taste is sweet,
cream of the crop;
before I lose my salad,
the hustle must stop.

God's Mistake

God's only mistake was creating emotion;
love ruins a man that's bound
by devotion.

Turns him weak to see the face;
with justified superiority, he should know
his place.

With impressive splendor and dazzling eyes,
it's the most expensive of gems he'll die
to buy.

But we're often betrayed by those closest to heart—
that's been my point from the
very start.

Stormy Seas

Taken for granted,
a lingering kiss.

Loved and lost,
like a hazy mist.

Assiduously sacrificed,
losing the soul.

Fragile and waving,
taking a toll.

A wave of calm,
stormy seas.

Call of death,
strangled pleas.

Source of solace,
borrowed time.

Forgotten memories,
a banished mind.

Ulterior motive,
lined in chalk.

Unbearable guilt,
subliminal talk.

Quivering Lips

Thunderous cries of anguish fan the flames,
blind insanity in black
despair with devilish names.

A tirade of anger paired with heart-wrenching sadness,
quivering lips with gnashing teeth,
a baffling madness.

I beat on my chest like I'm covered in flames;
I'm built for war,
you're built for games.

I do not care when I walk into battle;
I steadily progress,
utilizing the rabble.

My obligation to wreak havoc, 'tis a given;
this excursion through chaos makes my heart
worth living.

In an avalanche of pain, riveted, I'll stay,
making my bed,
it's with you I lay.

Hell to Pay

With rage burning brighter
than the sun on a summer's day,
I am the storm of storms,
and there is hell to pay.

Impetuous demands hold me tight
with a vise-like grip;
on a starry night with a taste for war,
blood does drip.

Crouched and snarling,
clenched for the fight,
purloined my amusement,
deprived of the sight.

Mordant interest,
glamorous and cruel;
curiosity sparked,
luring the fool.

Minor miracles chimed in the dark;
tiptoe to safety
from the beast
and its mark.

The Hunt

Finally free to forget the feeling
and my heart grows cold once again,
mischievous inflictions in the bowels of hell
is where I begin.

Your gullible acts and ridicule
have made me flee;
like a dissipated mist your rebellious sarcasm
casts an evil glee.

Deformed and contorted now,
revealing your hate;
the potential I see,
you've used as bait.

Melting towards the sky,
my soul is ripped;
your pronouncement of love
comes poison-tipped.

Now your blade protrudes
from back to front;
glistening in the flames,
my heart was the hunt.

Absurd Conundrums

Is too much love
as bad as no love at all?
—especially in a world
where loyalty is law?

Picasso of my time,
but only with words.
An abstract lyricist,
the conundrum's absurd

You mess with me
and you're gonna get beat.
An excellent flavor, but
damn sure not sweet.

This obnoxious context easily merged;
like electric currents the power surged.
Quaintly woven with a tentative touch;
with an iron fist, this crown I clutch.

Walled Away

Revenge is my mistress
and inflecting pain is her goal;
with the hint of a smile
and a gleam in her eye,
she will take your soul.

The embarcation of misery,
in her perfunctory way,
inhaling her aroma
while begging her to stay.

Anger creates deception
that's walled away from trust;
the sense of distance
from your soul
can't compare to the lust.

So prattle about as she strips you to the bone;
her smile is false,
she holds no love—
this she has shown.

Black as death is her heart
just look inside.
Run, if you can.
Lock the doors, she's coming—
so hide!

Premonitions

Inflaming my mind with the lies that you've told,
your deviating touch has also grown cold.
What once was pristine has now become sailed;
disabused and abandoned my heart has been failed.
A fetid stench permeating the hole,
from where my love died and with it my soul.
The fissures you left when you walked away,
with strategy set for the games you play.
Give the illusion that you really care,
but the premonition's clear that you're not there.

First of the Fallen

Wear the crown you claim
on the throne of lies,
but heed the warnings from
a past that cries.

With one foot in the gutter
and the other in the grave,
when Karma comes calling
the first of the fallen are the brave.

The war that rages within
you can easily be won
by planting flowers on the grave of hate
growing in the sun.

Live for the aroma of love,
forgetting the stench of despair;
this can easily be done as if
it's floating in the air.

Heroic Resolve

Feel the depths of love within my kiss;
for you, I yearn and clearly miss.
Vibrant in color with a burst of warmth,
a watery image only beauty can warrant.
My heart does race whenever you're near,
the sound of your voice I can't wait to hear.
With a hint of peace and heroic resolve,
compassion is relished, the sunshine dissolved.
It is no more the skies turned grey,
and I scream at the heavens to show me the way.
These pangs of guilt, mocking and cruel;
battle cries of love follow the rule.
My heart has wilted in utter dismay;
the feeling is scarce, yet won't go away.

Pearl Harbor

December 7th, a day that heroes were forged
in the fires of battle
and consumed by those lost and entombed.
A day the skies rained men and
machines alike, leaving the sea red
with blood from the fight.
It's the day the red dots flew low,
to our surprise,
ultimately consigning
their own demise.
From the festering anger left in the wake,
it's the great horizons
we planned to take.
The fires in life will scare or refine;
it seems it did both,
crossing that salient line.
Dropping our bombs with a radiant light,
the outcome was grim,
yet ended the fight.
So to our brothers avenged,
we made them pay.
Pearl Harbor is yours on this sacred day.

St. Louis

I'm in St. Louis where the windmills turn,
behind the fence where lifers yearn.
I see tempers flare and souls burn;
walk the line or it's your turn.
Where the guards watch with an eagle eye,
through the scope before you die.
So if that fence you try and climb,
in St. Louis laid in pine.
Hear the mirth of laughter in jest,
just before you're laid to rest.
So remember my words—I say it best:
walk the line on your quest.

Sentiments

Invisible in the mist like a stolen kiss,
your breathtaking beauty is what I'll surely miss.

Like a swan's caress, silky soft is your touch;
it's wavering mirage of your love, I just can't clutch.

When you are close my heart flutters—but not from fear;
in and out my chest heaves when you're near.

Meticulously kept and groomed so well, this radiant love,
deliciously destined to be the one sent from above.

And even though you tore me down; it was heartless,
I loved you then, I love you now, and always will—regardless.

You're my vision of loveliness, my sentiment has been shown.
How I feel, just ask around—everyone has known.

Not Enough

As I stare out the pane in pain,
I wonder if you'll ever see;
I wonder if you'll break free of your nightmare of lies
and come back to me.

I see you bleached by moonlight,
polished as marble;
warm and delicious, you have altered me completely.
You are a marvel.

The idea of losing you
has cured my unhealing heart;
one lifetime with you is not enough,
but at least it's a start.

So endearing and enchanting,
you've compelled my mind,
more angel than human with heartbreaking beauty,
and your voice did bind.

Physically compatible and
passionately in love,
in pale pink skies I hear the whisper of lips.
It was sent from above.

The Ravens

Sing your death song and die a hero in war
with an icy attitude,
the bloodthirsty implore.

The shock runs deep and explodes in your chest;
as reality sinks in,
it's harrowing at best.

Look at your comrades antagonized by the fight,
a hysterical pitch
from the garish sight.

That fetid smell from the slain;
the ravens have come
to lay their claim.

To the banished eating their fill,
wickedly digging
and pecking at will.

Repulsed as you are, you can't look away
from the unsettling sights
that are on display.

So as the snide linger and look today,
it's the rabid warriors
who are made to pay.

Pleading Eyes

When you're forced to live in the darkness,
you learn how to see within.
But the light can blind those pleading eyes,
sagaciously flaunting your demise.
A wretched squeal leaves a mark
on the soul of those who embark.
The pride you have is profane,
and the qualms you voice are in vain.
They are not heard—not a word—
but the quips that I give are absurd.
You are mundane, so must be slain;
succumb to the king, the one of bane.
With confidence built by combating the jealousy,
dramatically conniving and winning this legacy.

Feverish Chills

Legless corpses run on their hands;
in this quarry of pain, you can't make a stand.
Sharp wet teeth dripping with lust,
the taboo intruding like a rancid musk.
Feverish chills hinder the sane;
the abomination is spawned, living in bane.
Snarling rage a fabulous beast,
devoid of emotion preparing to feast.
Seething with hunger, ready to bust,
repressing the feeling—that of disgust.

Desecration of Love

My imagination soars when I
ruminate on the disappearance of my soul—
am I intellectually equipped for dealing with this toll?

The desecration of love so blatantly implied,
ultimately uncovering
everything you hide.

With a traitorous extraction indicating bane,
on the edge of hysterics,
burning in the pain.

In this traumatic travesty, you deviate your heart,
disrobing your feelings,
evicting every part.

This philosophy, which stems from the past,
keeps you from enjoying
all in which you'd like to bask.

Godsend

I can't and won't force this love
it is or it isn't sent from above.
If one thing is certain, He knows what's best;
my faith is unshaken, I do attest.

We are where we are, this is true;
I am who you want—who are you?
Like a thief in the night, no longer there,
I can't help but ask, do you even care?

It hurts my heart to think like this,
like being hit with an iron fist.
I need to know on which side you lie,
one way or another, ride or die.

I fear the answer and want to cry,
when I imagine your voice saying goodbye.
But until you do, the moon is my way
back to the apple of my eye.

My Heart

Your tantalizing beauty with lilies in your hair;
that lustrous smile, a country mile,
I can't help but stare.

I cherish every moment and always stay intrigued;
your kiss has me captive
more than is believed.

With lips sweet as honey and a heart made of gold,
my love is with you always
never turning cold.

I know you can't perceive what you don't believe;
as tangible as me,
this love we did conceive.

My heart I gave to you; it's forfeit through and through
so in this life become my wife
I need to hear you say "I Do!"

Gangster of Romance

The aroma of you is my symbolism of love,
embracing you from behind, wrapped in a hug.
An admirer of beauty, but only if it's yours,
with infinite tenderness healing your sores.
Delicately infused by my maiden of love,
obligated to this woman, I'll place no one above.
I'm a gangster of romance with sensitivity unbound,
fugitives of souls finally were found.
Receptive to your teaching in holding your heart,
my vow still stands, never will I part.
Even when we're grey, it's next to you I'll lay,
until the Lord calls me up, with you is where I'll stay.

Put It In the Air

I'm smoked and retarded because I put it in the air,
this pocket full of sunshine I can't wait to share.

Granddaddy purp and blueberry nugs,
for honey lemon haze, call your plugs.

Pineapple express or Gorilla Glue,
if you've got these, I'll match you.

But let's not forget our edible delights—
candies, cookies, and little brown bites.

Creeper's my favorite, but indica works,
let's not forget sativa—they all have their perks.

So who's got that funk?— and I mean the loud.
Let's put it in the air and blow out a cloud.

Sunlight on Soft Skin

Broken beams of sunlight in a shadowy nook,
crawling across your skin,
but I don't dare look.

For the secrets held beyond those eyes
would induce insanity—
hear my cries.

Surreal, it feels, but here you are,
infinitely close,
my shooting star.

Erupting within the purest glee,
abnormally captured
not willing to flee.

The endearing sound and burnt-orange hair,
with remnants of you
in the air.

In love, I've been, since the day that we met;
time may pass,
but I'll never forget!

Blinding the Sun

The skies bleed water, a soothing thrum;
white fire flashes,
blinding the sun.

Lulling and subtle, it strikes in stealth,
booming its might,
showing its health.

Its beauty is harsh—an arrogant pose,
like the thorn on a stem
found on a rose.

The grandest of sights you will see
looms in the skies
tactfully.

Spied at night for a better view,
streaks of light,
a severed hue.

The tempered calm when daylight pours,
spitting its rays
to warm the shores.

Twinkling Bright

An endless winter is what I face;
cold and alone, I have no place.
Love's disappeared without a trace,
just like your voice and your face.

Now I sit waiting for the pain to come,
but it's simply easier to come undone.
Some things in life I just won't do;
betraying your love is in those few.

Who would have thought I had a choice,
I was captivated the moment I heard your voice.
As the sun sinks down in a fiery sky,
giving life to the stars as I lie.

A shimmering mirage, twinkling bright,
gazing to the heavens on this night.

Death of Romance

There's nothing below, I wonder why,
the death of romance is in your eye.
Your heart's my rose—I'll treat it as such—
release the pain from their poisonous touch.

I can't continue unless you ask
to tear down the walls of your past.
Bumps and bruises, they do pass;
my heart is yours—never ask.

Among the rocks, I do shine,
discovered in dirt, the flawless kind.
I may shed tears, but cannot beg,
so tell me now: is love dead?

Think it through;
a gem, I am,
no longer hiding,
a king of men.

To Truly Care

The waning moon begins to rise,
full and beautiful
—what a prize.
Waterlilies floating without a care,
like expressive eyes
—see them stare.
A hint of honeysuckle in the air,
It's a funny thing to truly care.
In candlelight I see the shine
off the body that is mine.
Oh, what a sight given this night
in our bed and in flight.
To see you flushed brings a smile,
and taking your breath is my style.
With your hair billowing as if in flight,
You're cocooned in a halo of moonlight.
That throating purr comes from within
the woman I love until the end.

Boogeyman

There is no more pain to be seen in these eyes,
only hunger and hate
and a desire to despise.

Look into these pools of death and see,
that it is your demise
that is driving me.

Intimately held within my gaze,
as your last breath comes
it starts to haze.

I'll lay you down without a sound;
running rabid,
I am hell's hound.

The reaper of souls, if you can understand,
I plague your dreams . . .
I'm the boogeyman!

King of Suffering

Waves of torture, submerged in acid,
melted away, nothing to hold on to;
pieces of me shattered,
I've gone astray.

Mutilate my soul
and terminate my heart; on an endless ocean of grief,
my world
falls apart.

Screams rip through the night,
full of despair, past the boundaries of sanity
with a
fanatical stare.

Feeling boxed and unstable,
I'm not one to play, pain so deep you'd take
death with a smile
just to get away.

A deteriorating mind
like a perishing light, when I realized
my beloved
gave up the fight!

Standing Stagnant

Vehemently championed in the vanguard of distress,
I'm the king of suffering—
this I confess.
A wayward pedigree, pain hardened and sordid,
standing stagnant,
my mind's left torrid.
Fragility possesses a compassionless love,
eagerly hiding like a hand in a glove.
The fiery grip of a fading dream,
hindsight's 20/20, so it would seem.
Fabulous instincts of a frenzied soul,
your dwindling care vividly leaving a hole.

Radiant Shadows

To lose a memory
would be too much;
deciphering intrigue,
I've lost my touch.

Menacingly seeped,
induced into,
my brain is the rain
of venom's spew.

With eyes that gleam
the brightest blue,
with a mirth of laughter,
this joke's on you.

Radiant shadows
seething in blackness,
dormant fears
trickled with madness.

Sodden with shame,
a gravely dread;
like a candle in the rain,
love is dead.

The Suffering

The skies open up and swallow my soul,
like the suffering in life
that leaves a hole.
The things that bind me won't let me go--
saying is: you reap what you sow.
My shadow runs just like you,
away from me as if you flew.
This brokenness that isn't new,
sweeps me away like the wind that blew.
Now I sit and think about the shoe,
from the foot of a different view.
The painful caress of venom's spew,
it's the lingo I get talking to you.
The colors that show all of their hues,
tell of the choices that we choose.
So don't cry now, don't play the blues;
everyone's got to pay their dues.
Don't get it twisted or confused;
I don't give up—I do not lose!

About Joshua Stutzman

Joshua Stutzman grew up in a small town in the American Midwest. A fan of all art forms, he is an adventurer always eager to travel and explore. Father of three beautiful children, he is a poet and woodworker. *From Chaos, With Love* is his first published collection.

Fresh Ink Group
Independent Multi-media Publisher
Fresh Ink Group / Push Pull Press / Voice of Indie

⁂

Hardcovers
Softcovers
All Ebook Platforms
Audiobooks
Worldwide Distribution

⁂

Indie Author Services
Book Development, Editing, Proofing
Graphic/Cover Design
Video/Trailer Production
Website Creation
Social Media Management
Writing Contests
Writers' Blogs
Podcasts

⁂

Authors
Editors
Artists
Experts
Professionals

⁂

FreshInkGroup.com
info@FreshInkGroup.com
Twitter: @FreshInkGroup
Facebook.com/FreshInkGroup
LinkedIn: Fresh Ink Group

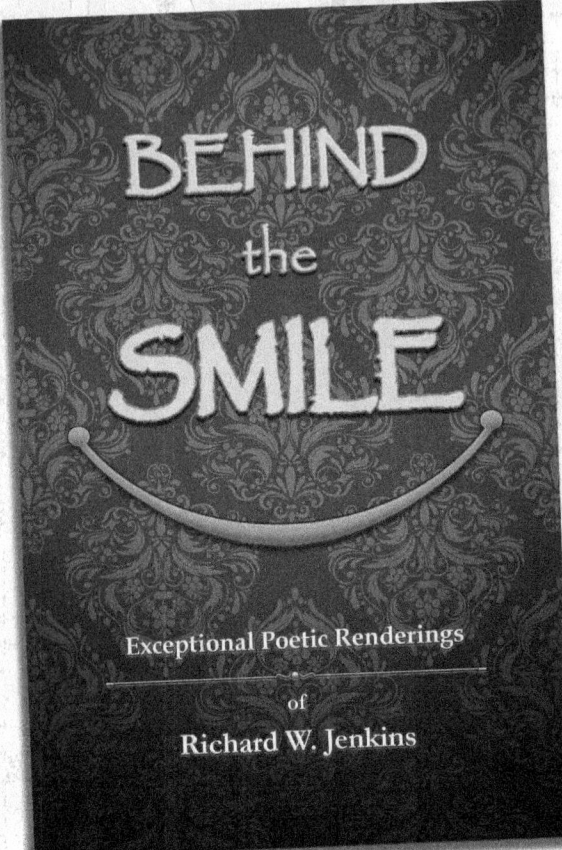

Hardcover

Softcover

All Ebooks

Worldwide

Come, take a peek Behind the Smile;
a world you've never known before
awaits your pleasures for a while ...
there's wonderment for you in store.

From Free Verse poetry to Sonnets, Ballads, and many more poetic forms and styles, this incomparably amazing collection of 145 selected poems by master poet Richard W. Jenkins is not your everyday smattering of poetic jargon. They will captivate and embrace your senses, taking you on a metaphorical journey of inner exploration and sheer enthrallment that will entice you irresistibly back into their pages—time and again. Aficionados will appreciate the author's breakdowns of the poems' 52 forms, including some of his widely used originals. This treasure belongs within easy reach of every poetry lover.

Whom could who feels what all we do
not yearn a deeper bite,
when each delicious taste we take
flavors our world just right?

Fresh Ink Group showcases 42 compelling prize-winners from its literary and genre short-story contests. Eclectic, daring, subtle, provocative, diverse—this wide-ranging collection by authors from across the USA and around the world transcends the limits of single-theme anthologies to explore the best of many styles and bold new ideas. Travel through time and space. Experience the Dust Bowl, a dying soldier's love, one distraught boy's mirror, the southern-farm snake, suicidal love lost, politicians run amok, a serial killer's lair, seductive sorcerous charms, a malevolent-house warning, inevitable moon-base death, the vengeful walking corpse, or a Holocaust child's hope, the lament of a life never lived... Discerning story-lovers are invited to listen for the voices of these newly favorite authors in Fresh Ink Group Short Story Showcase #1. Keep turning the pages to discover what unexpected delights beckon next.

www.ingramcontent.com/pod-product-compliance
Lightning Source LLC
LaVergne TN
LVHW051623080426
835511LV00016B/2149